— Donald Short

# A User-friendly Guide to *et. al. 1888 msg Study Committee*
## the 1888 Message

• the <u>everlasting</u> Gospel — will be preached to all nations
　eg "Gospel preached to Is. in wilderness"
　so why develop a <u>new</u> Gospel —

if anyone preaches any other gospel, <u>than the one I preached</u>
　let him be accursed — (cut off f/ Christ) (WARNING)

• what are acceptable + unacceptable ways of Bible
　study / interpretation ?

　　— the proof text method (how use/abuse) — the text.
　　— here a little, there a little,
　　　{ line upon line
　　　{ precept upon precept

　　— in his ical context — what mean to original
　　　hearers

　　— who is the intended audience ?

　　　I Cor 10  Bible written for us — upon whom the ends of
　　　the world have come.

# Some Other Books by George R. Knight

*1844 and the Rise of Sabbatarian Adventism,* editor

*Anticipating the Advent: A Brief History of Seventh-day Adventists* (Pacific Press)

*Early Adventist Educators,* editor (Andrews University Press)

*Ellen White's World: A Fascinating Look at the World in Which She Lived*

*The Fat Lady and the Kingdom: Adventist Mission Confronts the Challenges of Institutionalism and Secularization* (Pacific Press)

*I Used to Be Perfect: An Ex-Legalist Looks at Law, Sin, and Grace* (Pacific Press)

*Matthew: The Gospel of the Kingdom* (Pacific Press)

*Meeting Ellen White: A Fresh Look at Her Life, Writings, and Major Themes*

*Millennial Fever and the End of the World: A Study of Millerite Adventism* (Pacific Press)

√ *My Gripe With God: A Study in Divine Justice and the Problem of the Cross*

*Myths in Adventism: An Interpretive Study of Ellen White, Education, and Related Issues*

*The Pharisee's Guide to Perfect Holiness: A Study of Sin and Salvation* (Pacific Press)

√ *Reading Ellen White: How to Understand and Apply Her Writings*

*Walking With Jesus on the Mount of Blessing*

**To order, call 1-800-765-6955.**

Visit our Web site at www.rhpa.org for information on other Review and Herald products.

# A User-friendly Guide to the 1888 Message

**GEORGE R. KNIGHT**

REVIEW AND HERALD® PUBLISHING ASSOCIATION
HAGERSTOWN, MD 21740

Bible texts credited to RSV are from the *Revised Standard Version of the
Bible,* copyright © 1946, 1971, by the Division of Christian Education of the
National Council of the Churches of Christ in the U.S.A.  Used by permission.


This book was
Edited by Gerald Wheeler
Copyedited by Jocelyn Fay  and James Cavil
Designed by Willie Duke
Typeset: 11/13 Garamond


PRINTED IN U.S.A.


02  01  00  99  98          5  4  3  2  1


**R&H Cataloging Service**
Knight, George R.
    A user-friendly guide to the 1888 message.

    1. Seventh-day Adventists—Doctrinal Theology.   2. Righteousness by
faith.   3. SDA General Conference, Minneapolis, 1888.   4. Justification.
I. Title

                286.732


ISBN 0-8280-1325-X

Dedicated to my

wonderful wife, who

is such a blessing

in my life

1888 + its relat to:

a) Sunday laws + Relig liberty
   - how effected the ch –

b) the 10 horns of Dan. 7

c) the controversy over the law in Galatians

d) ea. G.C. session

e) later G.C. sessions

f) the events leading up to 1888 conference
   - how did EGW respond to

g) was there a conspiracy – to humiliate + side
   w/ ch leaders by EGW Jones, + Waggoner!
   ie why the gt Disappointment on part of theol leader
   as ⊃ Pharisees + Scribes in Chris day ?

   ⟹ + go by Sola Scriptura, but popularly held
      views that unwilling to relinquish
   + { when confronted ⊃ new interp + of Gospel/
     { law, + prophecy

h) R&F + law in Gal. – relat of

# CONTENTS

1. In a nutshell, what is the heart of the 1888 message?

2. Why was an understanding of the 1888 message of faith in an uplifted Saviour so important to Adventists in 1888?

3. Who were the key personalities in the 1888 struggle?

4. What part did the Sunday laws of the 1880s play in setting the stage for the contention at Minneapolis?

5. How did the differences of opinion over the 10 prophetic horns of Daniel 7 aggravate Adventism's leadership as it moved toward the Minneapolis meetings?

6. In what way did the controversy over the law in Galatians worsen an already difficult situation?

7. What role did the 1886 General Conference session and its aftermath play in the developing tensions?

8. How did Ellen White respond to the increasing tension among the denomination's thought leaders between 1886 and 1888?

9. How did fears of conspiracy bring a simmering situation to the boiling point?

10. What is known about the agenda of the 1888 meetings, and what major sources are available for people who have an interest in the Minneapolis General Conference session?

11. What did the discussion of the 10 horns of Daniel 7 contribute to the meetings?

12. What relationship did the law in the Galatians debate have to the presentations on righteousness by faith?

13. How did the impending national Sunday bill and religious liberty issues affect the 1888 meetings?

14. What can be learned about authority for deciding biblical/theological issues from the Minneapolis session and its context?

15. What was the "spirit of Minneapolis," and how did that attitude affect the reception of Jones, Waggoner, and Ellen White?

16. How did the so-called "California conspiracy" fuel the "spirit of Minneapolis" and its dynamic of rejection?

17. Why is Ellen White so important in understanding the meaning of 1888 for Adventist history and theology?

18. Did Ellen White have the 1888 message herself, or did she merely point to the messengers?

19. Is it true that Ellen White gave Jones and Waggoner one of the strongest endorsements of her entire career?

20. Did Mrs. White endorse other ministers in a way that would lead us to believe that God led them and that they had a special message for His people?

21. Why did Ellen White so frequently go out of her way to endorse Jones and Waggoner?

How did their
Theology / interp of
Scripture evolve?
1886 → 1888 → "1893, 1895 →'01

Relat of EGW's stmts re ?
& evthg Jones + Waggoner taught

22. Did Ellen White's enthusiastic support mean that she approved of everything Jones and Waggoner taught?

23. According to Ellen White, can too much attention be paid to the teachings of Jones and Waggoner?

24. What aspect of Jones and Waggoner's theology did Mrs. White so emphatically endorse?

25. Did Ellen White hold that it was essential that Seventh-day Adventists have knowledge of the *particular approach* of Jones and Waggoner to Seventh-day Adventist theology?

26. What is the most serious mistake that can be made in evaluating Ellen White's endorsement of Jones and Waggoner?

27. What was the greatest need of the Seventh-day Adventist Church in the 1880s?

28. Is it true, as some have claimed, that the 1888 message of righteousness by faith is a unique Adventist message?

29. Isn't it true that all Seventh-day Adventists believed in righteousness by faith before the 1888 General Conference session?

is people
believes VS
their understg of
with

30. What was Ellen White's understanding of the central meaning of the 1888 message? strengths / weaknesses

31. How did Waggoner view the process of salvation? VS square

32. How did Waggoner's view of salvation relate to the covenants?

33. Does salvation have conditions?

34. What is the relationship between correct theology and Christian love?

35. How does Seventh-day Adventism relate to the messages of the three angels of Revelation 14?

36. What was the standard interpretation of Revelation 14:12 before 1888?

37. What new insights on the meaning of the third angel's message emerged from the 1888 General Conference session?

38. What are the loud cry and the latter rain, and how has Adventist theology featured them?

39. In what way did Ellen White relate the loud cry to the 1888 message?

40. Did Ellen White claim that the latter rain had begun in either 1888 or around the time of the 1893 General Conference session?

41. What did Ellen White mean when she said that the loud cry had begun in 1888?

42. If the Adventists in 1892 and 1893 had the loud cry, where was the latter rain?

43. Given the fact that Jones, Waggoner, and Ellen White had such a poor reception among the leaders at the 1888 General Conference session, what steps did they take to spread their "most precious message"?

44. What was the response to the widespread preaching of Jones, Waggoner, and Ellen White?

45. What effect did the continuing Sunday law crisis have on the church?

46. What part did the Anna Rice excitement play in the latter rain expectations of 1893?

47. What kind of atmosphere pervaded the 1893 General Conference meetings?

48. What contribution did the 1895 General Conference meetings make to the evolving theology of Jones and Waggoner?

49. <u>What became of the four major Minneapolis contestants?</u> – E G W. – vs – G I Butler Gen. Conf. President
– Jones, A T      Uriah Smith. editor
– Waggoner, E G.

**THEOLOGICAL ISSUES RAISED BY THE MINNEAPOLIS MEETINGS**

Grt. claims

✗ 50. Was the 1888 message accepted or rejected? ?

8? ? intention of when 8pms truly committed

51. How many times did Ellen White <u>call for general</u> <u>denominational repentance</u> by the Seventh-day Adventist Church ⓐr its leaders in relation to the <u>rejection</u> of the 1888 message?

52. What part did discussions of <u>the human nature of</u> ✗ d) <u>Christ</u> play at the 1888 General Conference session?

53. How does the <u>theology of Ellen White</u> on the nature of Christ <u>compare</u> with that of Jones and his colleagues?

his Gospel will be preached all the world on earth or away of power then the end will come was the Gospel preached to the Antediluvians must $\bar{x}$ at top of ministry

54. Is there in Ellen White's writings, as there is in the publications of some Adventists, a <u>strong connection</u> between righteousness by faith and <u>final events</u>?

55. Is the 1888 message the message of <u>1888</u>, ⓐr the message of <u>1893, 1895</u>, or some other date? ie later revised + evolved?

56. What is the most important lesson for "<u>doing theology</u>" that can be learned from the 1888 experience? – Christian courtesy – open mind, calling → Jones (Dr Kellog)

1888  '93  '95 → Waggoner

**THE MEANING OF THE 1888 MESSAGE FOR TODAY**

→ EGW (Australia)

rest apart to the world.

Paul – reached the 7 story of the cross kept exact until ~ 1 P 1.7

31 → 34 etc

1. Adventism <u>needs</u> to <u>make</u> Jesus and His saving righteousness <u>central</u>.

2. Adventists need to recognize that <u>the good news is better than most people think</u>. – (loving people)

3. Adventist Christianity must move beyond the intellectual level to the experiential. unbalanced gift – mental vs social

④ Adventists <u>need</u> to understand <u>the true nature</u> of char-acter <u>perfection</u> both intellectually and experientially.

5. Adventists need to move beyond the spirit of Minneapolis and learn to <u>work together</u>.

? any needs for corporate repentance ?

? 11 did we miss the real msg / emphasis of R & F – Rtes of Chr.

6. Adventism needs to put the Bible at the very center of its theological methodology.

7. In studying the 1888 message, Adventists need to focus on those aspects of the theology of Jones and Waggoner that Ellen White explicitly commended.

8. Adventism needs to recapture the centrality of the third angel's message to its identity and forcefully preach a balanced message of law and gospel in their end-time context.

9. Adventists need to quit bickering with each other over the 1888 message and focus their energies on preaching the messages of the three angels to all the earth.

*Stop in fighting + preach to the world*

*- vs - is it nec/ to get it rt. 1st?*

*Avoid ⟶ The bus of Jews —*

*∫ we too need*
*to receive Christ*
*when He is preached*
*to us*

*• 1st preached to them*
*• but later taken to the*
  *world*
*• result is g'd jealousy.*

# A WORD TO THE READER

Seventh-day Adventists continue to view the 1888 General Conference session as a crucial turning point in their theological development. Though lasting less than a month, the Minneapolis meetings (October 17 through November 4) and the ministerial institute that preceded them (October 10 through 16) have changed the shape of Adventism. Yet Adventists more than 100 years later still find themselves divided over the meaning and significance of the 1888 meetings.

*A User-friendly Guide to the 1888 Message* raises 56 questions and sets forth nine propositions about the significance of the Minneapolis General Conference session for our day. Beyond that, the book presents answers that help unlock both the historical and theological implications of the most controversial General Conference session in the denomination's history. The questions and answers cover a wide spectrum of issues that surround the 1888 event.

Those familiar with my earlier work will realize that this is not the first time I have written on the topic. A decade ago I published *From 1888 to Apostasy: The Case of A. T. Jones (1987)*. Jones, of course, was one of the two major proponents of the so-called new truths set forth at the Minneapolis meetings. As such, *From 1888 to Apostasy* covered both Jones's life and the 1888 General Conference session.

*Angry Saints: Tensions and Possibilities in the Adventist Struggle Over Righteousness by Faith* (1989) followed that volume. I developed *Angry Saints* as a series of lectures I presented to the Annual Council of the General Conference of Seventh-day Adventists in Nairobi, Kenya, for the centennial of the Minneapolis meetings in October 1988. Two of those lectures I also gave at the centennial commemoration sponsored by the North American Division in Minneapolis in early November 1988. *Angry Saints* focused strictly on the 1888 General Conference session and pushed beyond the Jones biography in interpreting the theological significance of the meetings. Areas of special contribution were the relationship of the message of 1888 to the third angel's message, the meaning of the loud cry, and the proper use of authority in deciding theological controversy.

By the time I had completed those volumes, I had come to recognize that the history of the 1888 event was not an end in itself. Rather it was a means to an end. I soon realized that the core message of Minneapolis was to uplift the Bible and to uplift Jesus and what it means to be saved by Him. As a result, I began to examine what Jesus did *for us* on the cross and what He is willing to do *in us* in our daily lives. Those studies led to the publication of *My Gripe With God: A Study in Divine Justice and the Problem of the Cross* (1990), *The Pharisee's Guide to Perfect Holiness: A Study of Sin and Salvation* (1992), and the sermons I presented to the 1992 Annual Council of the General Conference entitled *I Used to Be Perfect: An Ex-legalist Looks at Law, Sin, and Grace* (1994).

Each of the above volumes presented themes highlighted at the Minneapolis session with its focus on God's great plan for saving humanity. But that emphasis, as I understand the implications of the 1888 meetings, centered on only one facet of the contribution of the 1888 session. Other important facets had to do with uplifting Jesus and Bible study. Those emphases led in my interest in developing *Matthew: The Gospel of the Kingdom* (1994), *Walking With Jesus on the Mount of Blessing* (the daily devotional for 1997), and my involvement as general editor of *The Abundant Life Bible Amplifier*—a 44-volume commentary series that will (when completed) lead people through a study of each book of the Bible.

As you can see from the above, the Minneapolis General Conference session of 1888 has changed my intellectual and scholarly life. But beyond that, and more important, it *has* greatly transformed my daily walk with Jesus. *I have discovered that the gospel is truly "good news."* It is my hope that the studies presented in *A User-friendly Guide to the 1888 Message* will not only enrich the lives of its readers but also *drive them* to a deeper study of God's Word and the great plan of salvation.

The aim of this book is to be user-friendly in the sense that it breaks down its subject matter into manageable segments through its use of a question-and-answer format. While I have written the book to be read through in its entirety, I have also developed it with those in mind who need a handy reference volume to answer the many questions raised by the topic. Thus it can be thought of as a "user-friendly handbook" to a variety of topics related to the Minneapolis conference.

*A User-friendly Guide to the 1888 Message* builds upon my previous writings on the subject, but does not do so in a wooden way. During the past 10 years my understanding has continued to develop. As a result, I have modified some of my earlier ideas and have enriched others in the present work. Thus the present book is not a mere rehash of my previous treatments of the topic, but a genuine advance in understanding. (As such, it presents much that *From 1888 to Apostasy* and *Angry Saints* did not contain. That is particularly true of the theological aspects of the Minneapolis session. Thus such areas as the significance of the covenants, corporate repentance, the acceptance or rejection of Jones and Waggoner's message, and the centrality of Ellen White for our understanding of the meaning of the 1888 message find a breadth of treatment lacking in my previous books on the Minneapolis General Conference session.) The exact words of Waggoner on the great themes of salvation also find a greater emphasis in this volume. On the other hand, many topics treated in my prior works on the Minneapolis meetings have more detailed treatment in those books, while some topics that they covered are absent altogether in the present book.

While I have supplied documentation in *A User-friendly Guide to the 1888 Message* for most of its main points, fuller documentation is usually available when the same topics have been treated in *From 1888 to Apostasy* and *Angry Saints*. Of course, the present volume includes topics not covered in my prior works, and it also adds new information on topics previously discussed.

In those cases, for obvious reasons, referral to my other volumes on the topic will be less beneficial.

As in my previous books, I am indebted to other people for their inspiration, insight, encouragement, and hard work. I would particularly like to thank Bonnie Beres for entering my manuscript into the computer; to Michael L. Knecht and Woodrow Whidden for sharing aspects of their own research with me; to "Woody" again for reading through the manuscript; to editors Gerald Wheeler and Jeannette R. Johnson, who saw the manuscript through the publication process; and to the administration of Andrews University, for providing financial support and time for research and writing.

My prayer is that *A User-friendly Guide to the 1888 Message* will be a blessing to its readers as they <u>wrestle</u> with some of <u>the greatest themes of the Bible</u>, <u>Adventist</u> history, and <u>life itself</u>.

George R. Knight
Andrews University
Berrien Springs, Michigan

*persons grow (even scholars) as they wrestle c̄ Divine Truth.*

*do - Jones + Waggoner have anything <u>new</u> to offer us today?*

# LIST OF ABBREVIATIONS

| | |
|---|---|
| **AGD** | Arthur G. Daniells |
| **ATJ** | Alonzo T. Jones |
| **ATR** | Asa T. Robinson |
| **BE** | *Bible Echo* |
| **CE** | C. Eldridge |
| **CEH** | Claude E. Holmes |
| **CMR** | C. McReynolds |
| **COL** | *Christ's Object Lessons* |
| **CPB** | Calvin P. Bollman |
| **CT** | *Counsels to Parents, Teachers, and Students* |
| **DAR** | Dores A. Robinson |
| **DKS** | Donald K. Short |
| **DTJ** | Dan T. Jones |
| **Ed** | *Education* |
| **1888 Materials** | *The Ellen G. White 1888 Materials* (4 vols.) |
| **EGW** | Ellen G. White |
| **EJW** | Ellet J. Waggoner |
| **EW** | *Early Writings* |
| **GAI** | George A. Irwin |
| **GC** | *The Great Controversy* |
| **GCB** | *General Conference Bulletin* |
| **GCT** | George C. Tenney |
| **GIB** | George I. Butler |
| **GRK** | George R. Knight |
| **GW** | *Gospel Workers* |
| **HJA** | H. J. Adams |
| **HM** | *Home Missionary* |
| **JEW** | James Edson White |
| **JHK** | John Harvey Kellogg |
| **JHW** | Joseph Harvey Waggoner |

| JNL | John N. Loughborough | *pioneer author* |
| JSW | Judson S. Washburn | |
| LFT | L. F. Trubey | |
| LHC | L. H. Crisler | |
| LTN | LeRoy T. Nicola | |
| MS, MSS | manuscript, manuscripts | |
| MW | Mary White | |
| NB | notebook | |
| OAO | Ole A. Olsen | |
| PP | *Patriarchs and Prophets* | |
| PT | *Present Truth* | |
| RAU | R. A. Underwood | |
| RH | *Review and Herald* | |
| RJW | Robert J. Wieland | *"discoverer of modern 1888 matters"* |
| RMK | Robert M. Kilgore | |
| SC | *Steps to Christ* | *what do they mean what is this msg?* |
| SM | *Selected Messages* (3 books) | |
| SNH | Stephen N. Haskell | |
| SP | *The Spirit of Prophecy* (4 vols.) | |
| ST | *Signs of the Times* | |
| T | *Testimonies for the Church* (9 vols.) | |
| TGB | Taylor G. Bunch | |
| TM | *Testimonies to Ministers and Gospel Workers* | |
| US | Uriah Smith | |
| WAM | W. A. McCutchen | |
| WAS | William A. Spicer | |
| WCW | William C. White | *son* |
| WI | William Ings | |
| WMH | William M. Healey | |
| WWP | William Warren Prescott | *W W Prescott* |
| YI | *Youth's Instructor* | |

# CHAPTER 1

# OVERVIEW: THE CRUCIAL IMPORTANCE OF THE 1888 MESSAGE

*see also Paleadale Mtgs.*

One of the greatest theological "events" in Seventh-day Adventist history took place in Minneapolis, Minnesota, during October and November 1888, at the annual meeting of the General Conference. This chapter will provide a concise overview of the significance of the meaning of the 1888 message. Subsequent chapters will expand upon that meaning and the events surrounding it.

## 1. In a nutshell, what is the heart of the 1888 message?

*TM 91-93pp*
*— E.G. White*

*more than a prophet, a msgr.*

*modern (prophets)*

Probably the best summary of the meaning of the 1888 message appears in *Testimonies to Ministers*, pages 91 through 93. In that passage Ellen White notes that "the Lord in His great mercy sent a most precious message to His people through Elders Waggoner and Jones. This message was to bring more prominently before the world the uplifted Saviour, the sacrifice for the sins of the whole world. It presented justification through faith in the Surety; it invited the people to receive the righteousness of Christ, which is made manifest

*Justification (thr faith) → vehicle · in the SURETY*

*invited people to receive — The R. of Chr*

*made manifest in obed. to all God's com's*

19

*the fact that God has a law is not recognized by many Chris today, alth/ they recognize laws of gov'te their need to protect society.*

A USER-FRIENDLY GUIDE TO THE 1888 MESSAGE

*, the fruit of love.*

in obedience to all the commandments of God. Many had lost sight of Jesus. They needed to have their eyes directed to His divine person, His merits, and His changeless love for the human family. All power is given into His hands, that He may dispense rich gifts unto men, imparting the priceless gift of His own righteousness to the helpless human agent. This is the message that God commanded to be given to the world. It is the third angel's message, which is to be proclaimed with a loud voice, and attended with the outpouring of His Spirit in a large measure.

"The uplifted Saviour is to appear in His efficacious work as the Lamb slain, sitting upon the throne, to dispense the priceless covenant blessings, the benefits He died to purchase for every soul who should believe on Him. John could not express that love in words; it was too deep, too broad; he calls upon the human family to behold it. Christ is pleading for the church in the heavenly courts above, pleading with those for whom He paid the redemption price of His own lifeblood. Centuries, ages, can never diminish the efficacy of this atoning sacrifice. The message of the gospel of His grace was to be given to the church in clear and distinct lines, that the world should no longer say that Seventh-day Adventists talk the law, the law, but do not teach or believe Christ.

"The efficacy of the blood of Christ was to be presented to the people with freshness and power, that their faith might lay hold upon its merits. As the high priest sprinkled the warm blood upon the mercy seat, while the fragrant cloud of incense ascended before God, so while we confess our sins and plead the efficacy of Christ's atoning blood, our prayers are to ascend to heaven, fragrant with the merits of our Saviour's character. Notwithstanding our unworthiness, we are ever to bear in mind that there is One that can take away sin and save the sinner. Every sin acknowledged before God with a contrite heart, He will remove. This faith is the life of the church. As the serpent was lifted up in the wilderness by Moses, and all that had been bitten by the fiery serpents were bidden to look and live, so also the Son of man must be lifted up, that 'whosoever believeth in Him should not perish, but have everlasting life.'

"Unless he makes it his life business to behold the uplifted Saviour, and by faith to accept the merits which it is his privilege to claim, the sinner can no more be saved than Peter could walk upon the water unless he kept his eyes fixed steadily upon Jesus. Now, it has been Satan's determined purpose to eclipse the view of Jesus and lead men to look to man, and trust to man, and be educated to expect help from man. For years the [Seventh-day Adventist] church has been looking to man and expecting much from man, but not looking to Jesus, in whom our hopes of eternal life are centered. Therefore God gave to His servants [Jones and Waggoner] a testimony that presented the truth as it is in Jesus, which is the third angel's message, in clear, distinct lines."

That was a long quotation, but it may be one of the most important in Adventist history. At this point it would be helpful if you went back over it and listed and/or underlined the points that Ellen White said were important in the 1888 message of Jones and Waggoner.

Even though your list (or underlined points) may differ a bit from the one that follows, they will probably be quite close in what they highlight. At the very least Ellen White was emphasizing the following points in the "most precious message" of Waggoner and Jones:

- *The uplifted Saviour.*

- *Justification by faith in Jesus.*

- *The connection between the righteousness of Christ and obedience to God's commandments.*

- *The need for Adventists to focus on Jesus.*

- *That Christ's righteousness or righteousness by faith has an intimate relationship to the third angel's message of Revelation 14:9-12.*

- *That Christ died in our place as an atonement for sin.*

✗ affirms the *subst / Substan* of Christ for me, un " 1 T. Sp. 'sanswer was to whether you believe it n not, ch, 21 died, for your sins "

*[handwritten: as result of uplifting ch 2]*

*[handwritten: ✱]* • That Jesus has special "covenant blessings" for His children.

*[handwritten: unbalanced msg]* • That Adventists had been emphasizing the law but neglecting Jesus and the importance of faith in His sacrifice for us. *[handwritten: ∴ we need to preach/teach more of Chs) + His excellent merits that they]*

*[handwritten: GRACE atmosphere p lost of text]* • That faith in the merits of the uplifted Saviour "is the life of the church." *[handwritten: may be appropriated to us!]* *[handwritten: Spirit of God]*

• That Satan's aim has been to move the eyes of the church away from Jesus and His merits and to focus the church's theology on human effort.

• That God raised up Jones and Waggoner to redirect the gaze of Adventists to Jesus, to faith in His sacrifice and merits, and to the relationship between salvation by faith and the message of the third angel. *[handwritten: also to bring Chs's sac for sin more prominent bef/ the World.]*

By this time you may be wondering what all the fuss is about. After all, isn't the above list pretty much at the heart of the very essence of Protestant Christianity? Why, you may be thinking, was such a message so problematic and troubling to some Adventists in 1888?

The answer to that question we will find in Seventh-day Adventist history between 1844 and 1888. It is to that topic that we now turn.

## 2. Why was an understanding of the 1888 message of faith in an uplifted Saviour so important to Adventists in 1888?

That question points back to the early decades of Adventism. Seventh-day Adventist theology consists of two types of related truth. The first category includes those doctrines Adventists share with other Christians, such as salvation by grace alone through faith, the importance of the Bible, the historic role of Jesus as the world's Saviour, and the efficacy of prayer.

The second doctrinal category includes those teachings distinctive of Seventh-day Adventist theology. Included are the sev-

*[handwritten: Prob. = Balanced Msg. Emph upon "Grace" or faith principle → leads to presumption or ch = over to Spiritualism]*

*2 categories of doctrines: 1) Those shared truths c
other Protestant Denom'. +
2)nd grp = distinctive truth
to Sd A Ch/*

OVERVIEW

enth-day Sabbath, the premillennial Second Coming, conditional immortality, and the judgment messages of Daniel 7 and 8 and Revelation 14.

Since nineteenth-century Adventists lived in a largely Christian culture, they tended not to emphasize those beliefs they shared with other Christians. After all, why preach saving grace to Baptists, who already believed it, or prayer to Methodists, who didn't need to be convinced on the topic? *ie proselytizing members f/ other ch'l*

The important thing, so the logic ran, was to preach the distinctively Adventist truths so that people would become convinced on such issues as the importance of observing the seventh-day Sabbath. As a result, Adventist evangelists would enter a community and publicly challenge the foremost minister to a debate on the nature of death and hell, the true Sabbath, and so on. Such an approach highlighted the Adventist distinctive beliefs. In an era before television and radio a combative method would draw a crowd in the small towns of the day. *debater spirit*

But other results were not so positive. For example, 40 years of such preaching led to a kind of separation between Adventism and basic Christianity. Thus Ellen White's plea in the passage we read above from *Testimonies to Ministers* that Adventists needed to preach the "message of the gospel of His grace" so that "the world [including the other churches] should no longer say that Seventh-day Adventists talk the law, the law, but do not teach or believe Christ" (p. 92). *see 1st Testimonies in 1880"*

The combative methods of Adventist evangelists led them to become debaters more interested in winning their point on the basis of a good Bible argument than in expressing love to those who differed from them. Thus Ellen White could note that "in presenting the binding claims of the law, many have failed to portray the infinite love of Christ" (1SM 371). To put it another way, Adventists had developed evangelistic techniques that often brutalized their opponents in the process. Even though they might be doctrinally correct, Ellen White suggested that they had the wrong spirit. *See I Cor. 13*

That wrong spirit, honed to perfect sharpness through repeated

*the emph. upon the law leads to a spirit of self dependence
that leads to self defensive attitudes when confronted by
R&F beef of I Cor 13 - Wischen Gottes - S lave I am nothing = scary.*

debates, would not be aimed at other churches during the Minneapolis General Conference session in 1888, but at other Adventist preachers who expressed different opinions from the majority. Mrs. White would label the false spirit that did so much to create disharmony in 1888 as the spirit of Minneapolis or the spirit of the Pharisees (see questions 15 and 16). • desire to control others • namely etc.

Thus by 1888 the denomination was ready for both a course correction in its theology and a course correction of a more experiential nature. Before examining the meetings themselves, we will first take a look at the events inside and outside the church that led up to the 1888 Minneapolis General Conference session.

*[The following handwritten margin notes appear on the page:]*

highlights: God designed that ATJ + EJW preaching would direct Adv. gaze to Christ, our High Priest →

• special Covenant blessing to God's people who preach the Surety — of Rt'ss of Christ as substitute for our unRteousNess — "filthy rags"

• SdA ch/ needs to preach + teach + live a balanced msg. — of preaching the still bindiing claims of God's law within the context of the Ev. Gospel + Jdgmt Hr msg & Dan 7   Rev 14 — 3rd angel assoc RxF, loud cry, et.al.
obed. to God should be taught + lived as a fruit of RxF

• RxF lays human pride in the dust so the debators spirit in ea. SdA is wrong spirit, = "phariseeism", a desire to control others by better Bible arguments etc. vs - need gr'tr reliance on H. Spirit

habit-letters RxF + EtGospel - 3rd angel - warning ag/ beast's image 1st angel

: we have here our sin cancel'd by the Gospel Furnishes the mind that H.Sp. = G-o-d's. Final Christ's inst.

# CHAPTER 2

Handwritten notes (top):

PRAYER - LORD, Help me to understand + accept your Word & R X P so I can "Keep the Com'ing of God" + have the "F. of Jesus" a F. in Jesus.

1) Preach the Surety → only Chi's RTSNK, perfect gives me a smur + flawed, assurance.

2) not a mere intellectual ascent at truth as in in Christ -

3) conversion is needed f purpose, Renew a Rt S.

4) See Steps to Christ

# MOVING TOWARD MINNEAPOLIS: PERSONALITIES AND EVENTS

To outward appearances the year 1888 began smoothly enough. "We turn our eyes to the future," Uriah Smith wrote in his opening *Review and Herald* editorial. "The prospect, year by year, grows clearer, the evidence surer, that we have not followed cunningly devised fables in making known the soon coming of the Lord. Prophecies are converging to their fulfillment. Events are moving with accelerated velocity. The Word of God is demonstrating its claims to truthfulness, and comforting every humble believer with the thought that the hope that is built thereon can never fail" (RH, Jan. 3, 1888).

General Conference president George I. Butler reflected the same mind-set. "We have much reason to thank God and take courage as we enter upon the year 1888," he penned in a circular letter to the Adventist ministry in January. Noting that *Seventh-day Adventists had "never taken a stand upon Bible exegesis which they have been compelled to surrender,"* he pointed out that "every year we have more and

*Jan. 1888*

*This looks pretty darn good*  "  1) Uriah Smith
                                      (R+H editorial )

                              2) G I Butler GC Pres.

A USER FRIENDLY GUIDE TO THE 1888 MESSAGE

{ circular letter to Adv.
{ ministers

more evidence that we are right in our interpretation of the great prophetic themes which distinguish us as a people" (circular letter, January 1888; italics supplied).

But even though outward appearances seemed to be calm enough in January 1888, a theological struggle second to none in the history of Adventism would burst into the open before the end of the year. In this chapter we will examine the personalities involved in that struggle and the events that led up to it.

### 3. Who were the key personalities in the 1888 struggle?

That is an important question, since personality conflict was a central element in the dynamics of the 1888 General Conference meetings. The major contestants were four in number, with George I. Butler (1834-1918) and Uriah Smith (1832-1903) representing the "old guard" establishment at denominational headquarters in Battle Creek, Michigan. Opposed to Smith and Butler were Alonzo T. Jones (1850-1923) and Ellet J. Waggoner (1855-1916), two young editors from California who challenged some of the cherished ideas of their older colleagues in the East.

By 1888 Butler had served as president of the General Conference of Seventh-day Adventists from 1871 to 1874 and from 1880 to 1888. Butler, in his better moments, could be quite honest about himself. Perhaps he made his most accurate and perceptive self-analysis when he wrote: "I . . . naturally [have] . . . too much iron in my nature" and not enough of the love of Jesus (GIB to EGW, Dec. 24, 1886).

Sensing early in the controversy that developed in the mid-1880s over the identity of the law in Galatians that he was too belligerent, Butler penned to Ellen White that he wanted "to be like Jesus—wise, patient, kind, tenderhearted, frank," with a "love of justice and fairness to all." He lamented the fact that there was a considerable amount of "human nature left in me" and that "I have great struggles with the old man." He wanted his old nature "to die. WHOLLY DIE" (GIB to EGW, Dec. 24, 1886; Nov. 16, 1886; Dec. 16, 1886).

Such a wish, however, was slow in fulfillment. Writing to J. H. Kellogg in 1905, Butler perceptively noted: "I am a pretty tough old customer, think for myself. You hit it pretty well once when you said, 'You might as well reason with a post as to reason with Elder Butler, when he gets his stakes set.' That is about so, always remembering that I try to be pretty careful before I set my stakes. Then it is pretty hard for me to root them out" (GIB to JHK, July 4, 1905). It was that unfortunate trait that drove Butler to fight to the bitter end over the issue of the law in Galatians in 1888. No wonder Emmett K. Vande Vere titled his biography of Butler *Rugged Heart.*

One final characteristic of Butler that we should note before moving on was his understanding of leadership. He believed in no uncertain terms that his very position as General Conference president not only mandated his ruling from the top, but also gave him "clearer views than others" (GIB to EGW, Oct. 1, 1888) on doctrinal issues and thus placed him in the role of theological watchdog for the church.

Uriah Smith, Butler's accomplice in power, had been secretary of the General Conference for all but three years since its beginning in 1863. Beyond that, Smith had been with Adventism's semiofficial periodical (the *Review and Herald)* since the 1850s, and by 1888 he had served for nearly 25 years as its editor. In addition, Smith was the denomination's unrivaled authority on prophetic interpretation. His *Thoughts on Daniel and the Revelation* was an Adventist best-seller among both church members and nonmembers alike. One of the Minneapolis-St. Paul newspapers noted in announcing his arrival for the 1888 meetings that "Elder Uriah Smith . . . has the reputation of being one of the ablest writers and speakers in the conference, and is, moreover, a profound scholar" *(Pioneer Press,* Oct. 17, 1888).

Like Butler, Smith viewed himself as a guardian of denominational orthodoxy. He succinctly stated his editorial policy in regard to some of the new ideas of A. T. Jones in 1892: "Having by long study, and years of observation in the work, become settled on certain principles, I am not prepared to flop over at the suggestion of every novice" (US to ATR, Sept. 21, 1892). That had certainly been his position in the face of Jones and Waggoner's "new theology" in 1888. Neither Smith nor Butler had the slightest inclination to "flop over" in the face of the teachings of the younger men from California. In fact, the exact opposite proved to be the case.

Certain characteristics of Jones and Waggoner didn't help matters. Mrs. White wrote a letter to them in early 1887 that sought to tone down their aggressiveness. "Elder [J. H.] Waggoner," she said, "has loved discussions and contention. I fear that E. J. W[aggoner] has cultivated a love for the same. We need now good humble religion. E. J. W[aggoner] needs humility, meekness, and Brother Jones can be a power for good if he will constantly cultivate practical godliness" (EGW to EJW and ATJ, Feb. 18, 1887).

To their credit, both Jones and Waggoner responded to her February 1887 rebuke in a humble manner. Waggoner replied on April 1 that her counsel was "timely" and "needed," and he lamented the fact that he had allowed a spirit of criticism and "controversy to creep in altogether too much" (EJW to EGW, Apr. 1, 1887).

Jones also expressed repentance for his part in the controversy, and for his defects of character. Compared with Waggoner, however, he would find it more difficult to put into practice the lessons he had learned regarding aggressive behavior. In the years to come Ellen White would repeatedly warn him against his harsh comments toward others. Having served as an Army sergeant on the frontier in the 1870s, Jones never lost the knack of treating others in commanding ways. His cocksure certainty that he was always right greatly aggravated that tendency. Such abrasiveness did much to set the tone for the Minneapolis meetings when he blurted out to the delegates in an early session that they should not hold him responsible for Smith's ignorance of certain historical details related to Daniel 7. Jones had done his homework, knew his facts, and sought to drive his point home.

While such an assertive stance toward a denominational patriarch at Minneapolis did little for his cause, Jones's fearless forcefulness undoubtedly aided him in the halls of the United States Congress in getting a repeated hearing on pending Sunday legislation that a more timid man might have failed to receive. Jones's career illustrates that he feared no one, thrived in the heat of battle, and never avoided conflicts over his beliefs. He could be just as tenacious as Butler and Smith when it came to standing for what he believed to be right.

Ellet J. Waggoner, coeditor with Jones of the California-based *Signs of the Times* and *American Sentinel of Religious Liberty,* had earned an M.D. degree in New York City in 1878. But not finding fulfillment in medical practice, he entered the ministry and received a call to editorial work at Pacific Press in 1884.

The major theological turning point in young Waggoner's life took place at a camp meeting at Healdsburg, California, in October 1882. During a discourse he experienced what he called an "extrabiblical revelation." "Suddenly," Waggoner reported, "a light shone round me, and the tent was, for me, far more brilliantly lighted than if the noonday sun had been shining, and I saw Christ hanging on the cross, *crucified for me.* In that moment I had my first positive knowledge, which came like an overwhelming flood, that God loved *me,* and that Christ died *for me.*"

Waggoner "knew that this light . . . was a revelation direct from heaven." He therefore resolved then and there that he would "study the Bible in the light of that revelation," in order that he might "help others to see the same truth." Because of that program, he noted, "wherever I have turned in the Sacred Book, I have found Christ set forth as the power of God, to the salvation of individuals, and I have never found anything else" *(Confession of Faith* 3, 4; *Everlasting Covenant* v).

It was Waggoner's "vision" that eventually led him into an indepth study of Galatians. Thus it is little wonder, given his starting point, that he found the *gospel in Galatians.* That discovery would bring him into direct confrontation with the Smith-Butler forces over their emphasis on the *law in Galatians* at the 1888 General Conference session.

The traditionalists' version of law-oriented Adventism apparently left Waggoner cold. He would never fall back from his Christocentric approach to theology, even after his departure from the denomination in 1906. Such steadfastness put him in league with the other three major contestants at Minneapolis. Even though his methods tended to be less abrasive than those of Butler, Smith, and Jones, Waggoner was a determined man who could hold his end of the rope in any theological tug-of-war. The strong personalities of the various participants helped set the stage for conflict at Minneapolis.

Before we move away from leading personalities, we should briefly note three other individuals who would play important roles in the 1888 meetings. The first is Adventism's prophetic voice, Ellen G. White. Even though Mrs. White held no official position in the Seventh-day Adventist Church, she was a major personage in the movement because of the denomination's belief in the validity of her call as God's prophet to His last-day people.

Throughout the 1880s she had sensed the need for more emphasis on the gospel aspect of Adventist teaching. And even though she had sought to maintain the role of a somewhat neutral mediator between the two contending theological parties between 1884 and 1886, by 1887 she had become increasingly vocal that Jones and Waggoner had something to say that the Adventist Church desperately needed to hear. Her support of Jones and Waggoner's gospel-oriented emphasis would turn to open advocacy by the end of the 1888 General Conference session.

W. C. White, Ellen White's youngest son, would also have an important part in the meetings, largely supporting Jones and Waggoner. Another personage of note was J. H. Morrison, president of the Iowa Conference and an expert debater. In the absence of Butler, who could not attend the Minneapolis meetings because of illness, Morrison became the major presenter of the law-in-Galatians position at the General Conference session.

4. **What part did the Sunday laws of the 1880s play in setting the stage for the contention at Minneapolis?**

Throughout the 1880s Sunday legislation and persecution grew in strength and scope. The problem surfaced in an explosive way in California in 1882, when the Sunday question became a major issue in the state's election—even to the point where some called for a third party with Sunday sacredness as its major platform plank. The consequences of the Sunday agitation hit Adventists when the local authorities arrested W. C. White for operating the Pacific Press on Sunday.

Although California soon repealed its Sunday law, the growing pressure for similar legislation across the nation spurred Seventh-day Adventists to action. Perhaps their most important move was to establish the *Sabbath Sentinel* in 1884 (*American Sentinel of Religious Liberty* after 1886) to publicize their reasons for opposing Sunday legislation and for observing the seventh-day Sabbath.

The scene of action shifted from California to Arkansas in 1885. Arkansas had had a Sunday law since 1883. It had originally contained an exemption for Sabbath observers, but the state had repealed the exemption in 1885—(allegedly to close saloons operated on Sunday in Little Rock by Jews.) Between 1885 and 1887 the state had 21 cases related to Sunday desecration. All but two had involved Sabbathkeepers, and the authorities had released the defendants in those two instances without bail and dismissed their cases. For the Seventh-day Adventists, however, bail ranged from $110 to $500 each—a stiff fine in an era when a living wage was about $1 a day. Meanwhile, the authorities had not arrested a single saloonkeeper. In addition, many of the accusing witnesses and informers had been working on Sunday—sometimes with the arrested Sabbath observers—yet no one molested them, even though the courts found the Saturdaykeepers guilty.

A. T. Jones concluded that "there could be no clearer demonstration that the law was used only as a means to vent religious spite against a class of citizens guiltless of any crime, but only of professing a religion different from that of the majority." Thus "the only effect of the repeal of that exemption clause was to give power to a set of bigots to oppress those whose religion they hated" (*Civil Government and Religion* 117-156).

By the late 1880s the focal point for Sunday prosecution had shifted to Tennessee, where local authorities would arrest several Adventists during the next few years. Some, including ministers, served on chain gangs as common criminals.

Events took on more ominous meanings for Adventists in 1887, when both the Prohibition Party and the Women's Christian Temperance Union openly sided with the National Reform Association in its drive to establish Sunday laws as a means of improving American morality. That same year saw Wilbur Crafts organize the American Sabbath Union for the same purpose.

Adventist eschatological excitement intensified in 1888 when Roman Catholic Cardinal James Gibbons "joined hands" with the Protestants by endorsing a petition to Congress on behalf of national Sunday legislation. The Protestants were more than willing to accept such help. "Whenever they (the Roman Catholics) are willing to cooperate in resisting the progress of political atheism," proclaimed the *Christian Statesman* in 1884, "we will gladly join hands with them" (*Civil Government and Religion* 58).

The high-water mark in the excitement on the Sunday issue came on May 21, 1888, when New Hampshire's Senator H. W. Blair introduced a bill into the United States Senate to promote the observance of "the Lord's day" "as a day of religious worship." Blair's national Sunday bill was the first such legislation to go before Congress since the establishment of the Adventist movement in the 1840s. Four days later Blair submitted a proposed amendment to the United States Constitution that would Christianize the nation's public school system.

Seventh-day Adventists did not miss the prophetic significance of the Blair bills. It was obvious to them that the forming of the image to the beast of Revelation 13, the giving of the mark of the beast, and the end of the world loomed close at hand. It appeared that American freedom stood on the verge of collapse. *Thus the eschatological excitement of the Sunday law movement served as one factor contributing to heightened tensions at the 1888 General Conference session.*

That eschatological crisis created an emotional atmosphere directly related to two other issues that would surface at the Minneapolis meetings. The first was the interpretation of prophecy—especially in the book of Daniel. The second involved the kind of righteousness needed for salvation—an important concern since the end of the world seemed to be sweeping down upon the church with great rapidity. That second issue would bring the function of God's law in the plan of salvation into focus as Adventists struggled over the identity of the law mentioned in the book of Galatians.

It is impossible to understand the high emotional pitch of the participants at the 1888 General Conference session without grasping the fact that Adventists felt, because of the Sunday crisis, that they already faced the end of time. S. N. Haskell wrote during the 1888 General Conference session that all that Adventists had taught for their entire history was now coming to pass, that their liberty as Sabbath observers would quickly be taken away, and that they might soon be bearing their testimony in courts and prisons. All they had taught for 40 years regarding prophecy pointed to their day (RH, Oct. 16, 1888). With that in mind, it is not difficult to see why some of the Adventist leaders reacted violently and emotionally when others of their number began to question the validity of the denomination's interpretation of some aspects of prophecy as well as its theology of the law. Such uncertainty, they reasoned, threatened the very core of Adventist identity in a time of utmost crisis.

**5. How did the differences of opinion over the 10 prophetic horns of Daniel 7 aggravate Adventism's leadership as it moved toward the Minneapolis meetings?**

One dynamic factor that set the stage for the 1888 meetings was the debate between A. T. Jones and Uriah Smith over the identity of the 10 prophetic horns of Daniel 7. Smith had been the acknowledged Adventist champion of prophetic interpretation for several decades. His *Thoughts on Daniel and the Revelation* served as the standard Adventist work on the subject. Jones, on the other hand, was a relative newcomer both to Adventism and to prophetic interpretation, but he was an avid student of both Scripture and history, as well as a rising star in the Adventist world.

The 1884 General Conference session had commissioned Jones to "write a series of articles gathered from history on points that showed the fulfillment of prophecy," a task that led him to study the book of Daniel. Smith initially expressed joy over the idea of Jones having the time to undertake a more complete examination of the 10 kingdoms of Daniel 7, but suggested that it would be a difficult task—somewhat like "hunting the pieces of a building" after it had been "struck by a hundred pounds of dynamite" (ATJ to US, Dec. 3, 1886; June 3, 1885).

The cordial relationship between the two men grew somewhat strained in early 1885 when Jones concluded that Smith's published list was incorrect. The younger man contended that the Alemanni were the tenth kingdom and not the Huns, as Smith claimed. Jones requested the older church leader to supply firm historical evidence for his positions, and he asked him to examine his own evidence for the Alemanni and comment upon it. Unfortunately, Jones received no answer to his first request, while Smith replied to the second one that he lacked time for the task.

As a result, Jones published his articles in the *Signs of the Times* without the *Review* editor having critiqued them. He then sent copies to Smith in October 1886.

The irate senior editor replied on November 8 that he would have to counterattack through the *Review,* since Jones had "scattered" his views "broadcast through the paper." In his reply Smith touched upon the nerve center of the problem. "If the Huns are not to be reckoned as one of the ten," he wrote, "I think we are yet ten percent short on the fulfillment of Dan. 2 & 7. You can readily imagine what the effect would be, if our preachers, after presenting the ten kingdoms as they have for the past forty years, should now change upon a point which has been considered so well established, that it has never excited a dissenting voice, nor called forth a challenge from anyone. *Thousands would instantly notice the change, and say: 'Oh! now you find that you are mistaken on what you have considered one of your clearest points; and so if we give you time enough, you will probably come to acknowledge finally that you are mistaken on everything.'* Thus the tendency would be to unsettle minds upon all points, a[nd] create confusion" (US to ATJ, Nov. 8, 1886; italics supplied).

Jones shot back an epistle on December 3. If Smith had been bold in emphasizing the reasons that Adventists should hold to the traditional interpretation during the current crisis, Jones would be equally trenchant. He wrote that "the real battle of the truth and for the truth has not yet begun" because Adventists had been "considered worthy of very little notice." But the Sunday crisis would change all that. Seventh-day Adventist beliefs in the end-time crisis would "become the principal subject of discussion in this whole nation. . . . Then our views are going to be noticed by the high in the land. Then every point is going to be analyzed and challenged by the scholarship and dignity of judges, statesmen, and the greatest in the land, as well as by the hypocrisy of religious bigots and the trickery of politicians. *Then it will be that our views will have to be examined by men who are acquainted with all the avenues of history,* and will have to pass the challenges that all these men can put upon the truth. . . . When we shall have to run down these lines through the history to show that we are right in our statement of the third angel's message, *we shall then to these men have to present some better reason for our faith than that 'it has been preached for forty years' or that Bishop Chandler said so.*" Such men, Jones continued, would require valid historical references. He closed by challenging Smith to correct the errors in *Thoughts on Daniel* that "every well-informed person knows" to be "not true" (ATJ to US, Dec. 3, 1886; italics supplied).

Smith returned the implied insult in mid-December, accusing Jones of "'ransacking of history'" in his attempt to prove him wrong. Once again the older man sought to rely on traditional authority. Jones replied on December 27 that traditional authority, "third-rate names," and commentators could not substitute for the "standard historians." "If," he wrote, "you have any reliable authority at all to show the kingdoms of the Huns" fits the prophecy, he would be glad to publish it in the *Signs* (ATJ to US, Dec. 27, 1886).

It is important to note that both Jones and Smith framed their justification for the importance of the 10 horns within the framework of the contemporary Sunday law crisis. That fact helps us understand why such a seemingly unimportant issue could generate so much heat. *After all, the Adventist interpretation of the Sunday crisis was a prophetic one. It hardly looked like a good time to be changing the denomination's position on prophetic interpretation.* Thus Smith and his allies dug in for battle. The issue of the 10 horns would receive special treatment at the 1886 General Conference session, but its major impact would surface during the Minneapolis meetings in 1888. By the eve of those meetings Butler would be thundering that Jones had proved himself to be a troublemaker by bringing up an interpretation "contrary to the long-established faith of our people taken forty years ago" (GIB to EGW, Oct. 1, 1888). The 10 horns would be a dynamic issue on the agenda of the Minneapolis meetings.

### 6. In what way did the controversy over the law in Galatians worsen an already difficult situation?

If the crisis over the 10 horns was intense, that generated by the issue of the identity of the law referred to in the book of Galatians was literally explosive. With the Sunday crisis right upon them it was bad enough to be tinkering with the validity of Adventist prophetic interpretation, but to be making major changes in the denomination's theology of the law could spell total disaster. After all, Adventists had a strenuous enough time upholding the perpetuity of the law in the hostile environment of late-nineteenth-century evangelicalism. Their Protestant contemporaries had them on the defensive. Many opponents even sought to do away altogether with the idea that the ten-commandment law was still obligatory.

One of Adventism's major arguments in support of the law had been its position on the two laws: the ceremonial, done away with at the cross, and the moral, which was eternal. That approach was so central to Adventist theology that Smith wrote in 1884 that "if it can be maintained that the distinction" between the two laws "does not exist, Sabbath-keeping at once disappears from the list of Christian duties. . . . No question, therefore, more vital to the interests of Sabbath-keepers can be proposed" *(Synopsis of Present Truth* 258). Perhaps the position's foremost champion was Dudley M. Canright, the denomination's most successful evangelist of the period, a debater who had successfully represented the denomination against other religious bodies on nearly a score of occasions, and the author of more than 20 books and pamphlets defending Adventist doctrine. His *Two Laws,* first published in 1876, was a major contribution to Adventist thinking on the law.

An important text that Seventh-day Adventists had to contend with was the "added law" of Galatians 3:19-25. For three decades Adventists had interpreted that law to be what they called the "ceremonial" law. Such an interpretation, Adventist leaders held, was important in guarding the perpetuity of the Ten Commandments. After all, did not Galatians 3:25 plainly teach that once an individual had faith, he or she was "no longer under a schoolmaster"?

The law in Galatians had become a controversial issue between 1884 and 1886 when A. T. Jones and E. J. Waggoner began to teach that Galatians had the Ten Commandments in mind rather than the ceremonial laws. Waggoner published their view in the *Signs,* and both men taught it at Healdsburg College in California. Many regarded the "new" interpretation as a threat to the very heart of Adventist theology—the continuing sacredness of the seventh-day Sabbath embedded in the moral law. In order to defend their position on the Sabbath in a hostile religious context, Adventists had protected their theology by interpreting the law in Galatians as the ceremonial regulations. Thus the church leadership perceived Jones and Waggoner as endangering one of Adventism's central theological pillars.

The General Conference forces, led by Butler and Smith, felt quite confident in their perspective because they believed that the church had settled the question once and for all back in 1856. Before that time many Adventists—including James White, J. N.

Andrews, Uriah Smith, and Joseph Bates—had held that the law mentioned in Galatians was the Ten Commandments. The issue had come to a head when J. H. Waggoner (E. J.'s father) published *The Law of God: An Examination of the Testimony of Both Testaments* (1854), which took the Ten Commandments view of the law in Galatians. In 1856 Stephen Pierce had challenged that position when he argued that the law in Galatians "was the law system including the ceremonial law." The participants in the discussion—including James and Ellen White—swung over to Pierce's viewpoint. Smith and Butler even went so far as to claim that Mrs. White had had a vision on the topic and had written to J. H. Waggoner that the law in Galatians could not be the moral law. While Smith and Butler never documented their claim, it is a historical fact that after the 1856 conference James White removed Waggoner's book from the market. For the next 30 years the church harmoniously taught that the law in Galatians was the ceremonial regulations (GIB to EGW, Oct. 1, 1888; US to WAM, Aug. 8, 1901; US to HJA, Oct. 30, 1900).

It was into that seemingly settled theological atmosphere that E. J. Waggoner shot his articles on Galatians. Butler, as president of the General Conference and defender of the faith, immediately felt concerned. During a visit to Healdsburg College in early 1886 he became quite incensed over Jones and Waggoner's efforts. "When we learn that the . . . view held by the minority is being vigorously pushed in one of our colleges among our Bible students and published to the world in the *Signs*," he penned, "I confess it does not please me very well" (GIB to EGW, June 20, 1886). That was probably an understatement of the depth of his emotions on the topic. The issue would soon become so important in his mind that he would come perilously close after the Minneapolis meetings to leaving the denomination of which he was president.

Just what was it that so bothered Butler and his friends about Waggoner's position on Galatians? Butler supplies a partial answer in his 1886 critique of Waggoner's *Signs* articles. He observed that the *Signs* had a large circulation and that it "comes under the observation of many of our ablest opponents." Its treatment of the law in Galatians was particularly important *"because the apostle's references to the law in this letter are used by our opponents as a strong support to their Antinomian doctrines." Thus Waggoner and Jones were providing "great aid and comfort" to the Adventists' anti-law enemies (The Law in the Book of Galatians 6, 7, 66; italics supplied).*

Butler supplied further reasons for the importance of the Galatians controversy in October 1888. By that time he viewed it as "the opening wedge" by which a "deluge" of doctrinal and prophetic changes were being "let in" to the Adventist Church. Beyond that, he claimed, it would "break the faith of many of our leading worker[s] in the Testimonies," since Ellen White had purportedly had a vision establishing that the law in Galatians could not be the ten-commandment law (GIB to EGW, Oct. 1, 1888).

Smith was one in heart and mind with Butler. For him, "next to the death of Brother White, the greatest calamity that ever befell our cause was when Dr. Waggoner put his articles on the book of Galatians through the *Signs*." If the denomination ever changed its position on Galatians, he flatly stated, "they may count me out," because "I am not yet prepared to renounce Seventh-day Adventism." He firmly believed that if the traditional position was incorrect, "then we have been wrong for the past thirty years, and Seventh-day Adventism has been developed and built upon error." Taking the ten-commandment view of the law in Galatians, he held in concurrence with Butler, "overthrows the Testimonies and the Sabbath" (US to EGW, Feb. 17, 1890; US to ATR, Sept. 21, 1892; US to LFT, Feb. 11, 1902).

Waggoner, on the other hand, believed (as did Jones on the 10 horns) that it was more important to be correct than to uphold an erroneous traditional interpretation. *"As we approach the end,"* he wrote, *"all the forces of the enemy will be concentrated"* upon the *Adventist interpretation of the law.* "Every point in our argument will have to be subjected to the test of the most rigid criticism."

"I know," he continued, "you will say that it will be a humiliating thing to modify our position on so vital a point . . . in the face of the enemy. But if a general has a faulty position, I submit that it is better to correct it . . . than to run the risk of defeat because of his faulty position." Waggoner personally saw nothing humiliating in a change of denominational interpretation. Such a modification "would simply be an acknowledgement that" Adventists "are better informed to day [sic] than they were yesterday" *(The Gospel in the Book of Galatians* 70).

We should note that both sides in the Galatians struggle justified their aggressiveness by relating it to the Sunday law issue. The same was true in their magnification of the 10 horns debate. Thus it is important to see the emotional battle that ensued within that all-important crisis context. Adventists believed by 1888 that they were arguing for the highest stakes and that they would soon face scrutinizing examination before the world's greatest tribunals of justice and scholarship as they refused to submit to the mark of the beast power as it related to Sunday laws.

### 7. What role did the 1886 General Conference session and its aftermath play in the developing tensions?

Butler sought to resolve the struggles over the law and prophetic interpretation by the end of 1886. During the summer of that year he had begun a campaign to rectify the disagreements—in favor of the traditional positions, of course.

His first line of attack involved writing a series of letters to Ellen White, who was in Europe, to enlist her aid against Jones and Waggoner, men who had been bold enough to advocate in print theological and prophetic viewpoints contrary to long-established Adventist positions.

To say the least, Ellen White's silence to Butler's repeated request (see question 14) greatly frustrated him. As a result, he had shifted to tactic number two by the end of August 1886. He would compose a "brief comment on the Epistle to the Galatians" on the topic of the law, since the *Signs* had put forth the subject "in the most public manner possible" (GIB to EGW, Aug. 23, 1886). His "brief comment" turned out to be an 85-page book entitled *The*

*Law in the Book of Galatians.* It proved to be a thorough attack on Waggoner's position. In addition to Butler's book, the denomination's leaders brought out a new printing of Dudley M. Canright's *Two Laws,* first published in 1876. The 1886 printing sported only one obvious change—the section on the law in Galatians had expanded from six to 24 pages.

Butler's third tactic was to utilize the 1886 General Conference session to put Jones and Waggoner and their "false teachings" in their proper place and thus get the denomination back on track. The General Conference president provided every attendee with a copy of his *Law in the Book of Galatians.* More important, he organized a theological committee to settle the issues of the 10 horns and the law in Galatians once and for all. E. J. Waggoner, Canright, Smith, and Butler served on it. However, Butler's hope for a creedal statement that would establish the truth on the controverted points for all time met with frustration. The nine-member committee split five to four. "We had an argument of several hours," he reported, "but neither side was convinced." The next question, he noted, "was whether we should take this into the conference and have a big public fight over it." Being an astute politician, he realized that such a move would only cause more trouble (GIB to EGW, Dec. 16, 1886).

The upshot of the stalemate was that President Butler had to settle for a compromise in which the delegates approved a resolution that "doctrinal views not held by a fair majority of our people" could not be made a part of the instruction in Adventist schools or published in denominational papers until they had been "examined and approved by the leading brethren of experience" (RH, Dec. 14, 1886). The regulation obviously had Jones and Waggoner, their editorship of the *Signs,* and their teaching at Healdsburg College in mind. The compromise, however, was never really effective—it merely put off the showdown to a later date.

Both Butler and Ellen White would look back on the 1886 General Conference session as that "terrible conference." While he noted that the meeting was one of the saddest he had ever attended, she pointed out that "Jesus was grieved and bruised in the person of His saints." She especially felt disturbed about the "harshness," "disrespect, and the want of sympathetic love in brother toward brother." The dynamics of Minneapolis were already in place (GIB to EGW, Oct. 1, 1888; Dec. 16, 1886; EGW to GIB, Oct. 14, 1888; EGW MS 21, 1888).

Perhaps the most visible casualty of the 1886 meetings was Canright—one of the denomination's most successful evangelists and a champion of the traditional approach to the law as interpreted by Butler and Smith. Canright had been in the center of the battle against Waggoner over the law and the covenants on the theological committee. In the heat of the debate he must have grasped the fact that Waggoner had a valid point. Unfortunately Canright came to believe that if the denomination was wrong in its traditional interpretation of the law, "their [the Seventh-day Adventists'] cause is lost." But instead of adopting Waggoner's view of the Ten Commandments as leading individuals to Christ, Canright dropped both the perpetuity of the law and Adventism. Later he pointed back to the debate over the law in Galatians in 1886 as a major turning point, after which he reexamined the Adventist position on the law for several weeks. He then laid his findings before the leaders at Battle Creek, resigned all his official positions, and asked them to dismiss him from the church. The leadership granted his request on February 17, 1887. That same day Butler wrote to Mrs. White that Canright had left over the results of his study on the "law question" *(Seventh-day Adventism Renounced,* 5th ed., 309, 50, 51; GIB to EGW, Feb. 17, 1887).

Butler stated in the *Review* that *Canright "thought that we were exalting the law above Christ." At this point Butler touched upon what would become the central theological issue of the meaning of the 1888 General Conference session.* Canright comprehended the problem in late 1886, but could not adjust his law-oriented theology to account for the truth of the gospel of salvation by grace through faith. He saw no option but to reject the law and join the gospel-oriented Baptists. Subsequently he would become the Adventists' most formidable opponent, publishing his influential *Seventh-day Adventism Renounced* in 1889.

The General Conference president found it "astonishing to us all how he could change so quickly and radically." He blamed it on Canright's unstable character (RH, Mar. 1, 1887). It is true that Canright had been erratic in his relationship to the church, but the evidence indicates that he had grasped the fact that the Adventist leadership was confused on the question of the covenants and had placed the law above the gospel.

While Canright understood part of the truth that Waggoner was seeking to present, Butler, Smith, and their colleagues held blindly to their traditional Adventism with its major theological problems that would become more evident in subsequent years. The loss of Canright over the Galatians issue should have awakened Smith and Butler, but his defection merely led them to dig their heels in deeper and to prepare for further battle. The apostasy certainly didn't help them soften their attitude toward Jones and Waggoner and the men's new theology that emphasized "the gospel in Galatians." To the contrary, it raised the old guard's emotionalism on the issue. After all, hadn't they predicted that the new teaching would bear such fruit?

Canright was not the only church thinker busy in the wake of the 1886 General Conference session. E. J. Waggoner, who Butler claimed had come to the conference "fully armed for the fray," penned a "letter," dated February 10, 1887, to Butler that later saw publication as the 71-page *Gospel in the Book of Galatians.* Waggoner's book was an extensive critique of Butler's *Law in the Book of Galatians,* which the denominational president and his supporters had distributed at the recent General Conference session.

### 8. How did Ellen White respond to the increasing tension among the denomination's thought leaders between 1886 and 1888?

Ellen White's pen was also active during the early months of 1887. One of her most important letters went to Jones and E. J.

Waggoner on February 18. In it she indicated that she had been looking for the testimony she had written to J. H. Waggoner in the 1850s on the "added law" of Galatians, but could not find it. She recalled that she had written "to him that I had been shown his position in regard to the law was incorrect," but that she could not recall exactly what was incorrect about it, since "the matter does not lie clear and distinct in my mind." Of one thing, however, she was certain. Adventists should present a united doctrinal front to the public. "Especially at this time," she said in an obvious reference to the vulnerability and visibility of the denomination in the Sunday crisis, "should everything like differences be repressed." Mrs. White definitely faulted the two young editors for making their positions public in the *Signs*.

Then she went on to claim that the various positions on the law in Galatians "are not vital points." Noting that it would take years to "wipe out the impressions made at our last conference [1886]," she said that she would refuse to attend another session if the leadership placed such issues as Galatians or the 10 horns on the agenda.

Moving beyond points that were "not vital," Ellen White highlighted what she considered to be essential. "There is danger," she emphasized, "of our ministers dwelling too much on doctrines, preaching altogether too many discourses on argumentative subjects when their own soul needs practical godliness. . . . The wonders of redemption are dwelt upon altogether too lightly. We need these matters presented more fully and continuously. . . . There is danger of keeping the discourses and the articles in the paper like Cain's offering, Christless" (EGW to EJW and ATJ, Feb. 18, 1887). Such themes would form the backbone of her writing and preaching at Minneapolis and throughout the 1890s.

Ellen White's letter was a definite rebuke to Jones and Waggoner for making divisive issues public in a time of crisis and for certain of their undesirable character traits. Both men replied positively, humbly apologizing for their public and private faults. One result of the interchange was that Waggoner withheld the publication of his *Gospel in the Book of Galatians*. The manuscript would not reach print until shortly before the 1888 General Conference session.

A copy of the letter reproving Jones and Waggoner also went to Butler. Ecstatic with its contents, he mistakenly interpreted it as confirmation of his position on the law. In his euphoria he wrote to Ellen White that he had really come to "love" the two young men, noting that he felt sorry for them. "I always pity those who suffer keen disappointment" (GIB to EGW, Mar. 31, 1887). Despite his "pity," Butler joyfully published an aggressive article in the *Review* of March 22 promoting his position on the two laws.

To put it mildly, Butler's use of her letter to Jones and Waggoner upset Mrs. White. On April 5, 1887, she fired off an epistle to Butler and Smith, claiming that she had not sent them a copy of the Jones-Waggoner rebuke so that they could use it as a weapon against the younger men, but that they should follow the same cautions in bringing disagreements into public. Now that Butler had publicly reopened the battle, she stated adamantly, Waggoner would have to have a chance to present his views publicly. While stating that the "whole thing is not in God's order," she called for fairness. That demand for fairness eventually led to the publication of Waggoner's book on Galatians and to the controverted points becoming major items on the agenda of the 1888 General Conference meetings.

As Mrs. White began to see the issues more clearly, she became more aggressive toward the high-handed methods of the Battle Creek leadership. "We must work as Christians," she wrote. "If we have any point that is not fully, clearly defined and [cannot] bear the test of criticism, don't be afraid or too *proud* to yield it. . . . *We want the truth as it is in Jesus.* We want to be filled with all the fullness of God, and have the *meekness* and *lowliness* of Christ." Accusing Smith and Butler of being in the same boat with the apostatized Canright, she claimed that she would "burn every copy" of his book on the two laws "before one should be given out to our people." In response to Butler's repeated request for her to settle the Galatians question by making an authoritative statement, she claimed that *"we want Bible evidence for every point we advance."* The themes Mrs. White stressed in her April 5 letter would be ones that she would continue to emphasize throughout the Minneapolis experience. By April 1887 she had a distinct view of the nature of the problem facing the denomination.

In her letter to Butler and Smith, Ellen White once again referred to the lost testimony to J. H. Waggoner, pointing out that her counsel may not have been on doctrine at all. "It may be it was a caution not to make his ideas prominent at that time, for there was great danger of disunion" (EGW to GIB and US, Apr. 5, 1887; italics supplied).

Butler and Smith disagreed with her recollection, holding that she had seen in vision that J. H. Waggoner had been wrong theologically. Thus both men claimed that if they were in error on Galatians, it would overthrow both the Sabbath and Ellen White's Testimonies—a position that harmonized perfectly with that of Canright. Such thoughts continued to develop as the denomination drifted toward the Minneapolis meetings in the fall of 1888 (US to ATR, Sept. 21, 1892; GIB to EGW, Oct. 1, 1888).

### 9. How did fears of conspiracy bring a simmering situation to the boiling point?

Early in 1888 W. C. White began to correspond with Butler regarding a ministerial institute to precede the formal General Conference session. He proposed several lines of study for the institute that included an examination of Bible doctrines. The General Conference president, in his replies, suggested that the 10 kingdoms and the law in Galatians should be included in the topics to be examined.

By that summer, however, the busy Butler had forgotten that he had ever made such a recommendation. As a result, W. C. White sought to convince him that nothing could be healthier for the denomination than for its differing leadership "to sit down together in a kind and Christian spirit and patiently hear each other present their views." After all, he noted, no one could prevent Adventism's opponents from examining its accepted points of faith, and merely relying on tradition would place Adventists in a position similar to that of the creedal churches (WCW to DTJ, Apr. 8, 1890; WCW to GIB, Aug. 16, 1888).

On August 5 Ellen White jumped into the debate over the ministerial institute. Her circular letter to the delegates was a rousing call to "search the scriptures," since "the truth can lose nothing by close investigation." The Adventist people, she suggested, would be "called before councils" and "be criticized by keen and critical minds." Many, including those in the ministry, were deficient in Bible understanding. They had relied too heavily upon the authority of the leadership and Adventist tradition. "We are not to set our stakes," she stated in an obvious thrust at the Smith-Butler mentality, "and then interpret everything to reach this set point." That was where the Reformers had left the path of biblical faith. *"The Bible,"* she proclaimed, *"must be our standard for every doctrine and practice.* . . . We are to receive no one's opinion without comparing it with the Scriptures. Here is divine authority which is supreme in matters of faith. It is the word of the living God that is to decide all controversies." She went on to point out that they needed to study the Bible "in the Spirit of Christ" without "giving sharp thrusts." All "pharisaism" was to be set aside, and "all assumptions and preconceived opinions are to be thoroughly tested" by Scripture.

Ellen White's August 5, 1888, letter reinforced her April 1887 call for fairness and equal time. Jones and Waggoner, she intimated in no uncertain terms, should have their hearing. Beyond that, she once again highlighted two themes that would become central to her at Minneapolis—the all-important authority of the Bible and the necessity of having the spirit of Jesus rather than that of the Pharisees (EGW to Brethren, Aug. 5, 1888; italics supplied).

In the face of such an open call for Bible study and Christian justice, Butler had no choice but to capitulate. In the *Review* of August 28 he announced the holding of the ministerial institute and the fact that it would explore the debated issues.

Butler's finally agreeing to the institute and the discussion of the points of controversy did not mean that he ever came to terms with the prospect in a healthy way. To the contrary, by the beginning of October, on the eve of the meetings, he had worked himself up into an emotional state and was close to a breakdown. On October 1 he penned a more than 40-page letter to Ellen White. The president of the General Conference accused her of betraying him and pinpointed her son as having played a particularly distasteful role in the conflicts that had shaken the denomination since 1884. Butler had never seen any justice in her April 5, 1887, letter, "and never expect to." As far as Jones and Waggoner were concerned, he had never observed "a more barefaced and defiant course on a controverted question." He regretted that he and Smith "did not just wade into them and show them up in the widest channels possible" when they had first put their ideas in print. In the days when James White had been president, "those young men would . . . have heard thunder around their ears . . . that would have made them tingle." White would have immediately gone "for them in public and private" and made them "regret such boldness." He would not have hesitated to expose such "young fledglings" through the pages of the *Review* (GIB to EGW, Oct. 1, 1888).

Butler did not get into such a dither by himself. A letter that he had recently received from William M. Healey, a pastor in California, fueled his reaction. Healey reported a meeting that had taken place between W. C. White, E. J. Waggoner, A. T. Jones, and other leading West Coast ministers in June 1888. They had met to study the Bible in relation to such issues as the 10 kingdoms, the law in Galatians, and prophetic events. While the meeting was apparently an honest Bible and historical study, Healey—in the emotionally charged atmosphere—trumped it up into a sinister plot by the Western leadership to force a change in the denomination's theology (EGW to WMH, Dec. 9, 1888; US to EGW, Feb. 17, 1890; WCW to DTJ, Apr. 8, 1890).

Healey's letter found fertile ground in Butler's emotionally exhausted mind. He had been smarting for 18 months from the letter

Ellen White had sent him in April 1887 regarding his wrong attitude to Jones and Waggoner and their views. Suddenly it all came together for him. Now he could see why W. C. and Ellen White had urged that he place the 10 horns and the law in Galatians on the Minneapolis agenda. Certainly here was a conspiracy of the first magnitude and a threat to the denomination's traditional beliefs. He therefore shot off a series of telegrams to the delegates at Minneapolis, warning them to "stand by the old landmarks" and not to give an inch to the California conspirators. As a result, his followers dug in for battle, desiring to protect both their president and the "old landmarks" (ATJ to CEH, May 12, 1921; EGW MSS 15, 2, 1888; EGW to MW, Oct. 9, 1888).

Thus the stage was set for disaster at Minneapolis. "We are in for it," Ellen White quipped a day before the meetings began (EGW to MW, Oct. 9, 1888; see also questions 15 and 16).

# CHAPTER 3

# THE 1888 MEETING: EVENTS AND DYNAMICS

The Minneapolis *Journal* of October 13 trumpeted the Adventists as "A Peculiar People Who Keep Saturday as Sunday, Revere a Prophetess, and Believe the End of the World Is Nigh." The October 19 *Journal* reported that the Adventists "tackle difficult problems in theology with about the same industry that an earnest man would assail a cord of wood." The newspaper might have added that they were also just about that gentle with each other in their theological dialogue. The aggressive spirit evidenced was just what Ellen White had feared might happen. But before examining that attitude and the events that brought it into the open, we should examine the agenda of the 1888 meetings.

**10. What is known about the agenda of the 1888 meetings, and what major sources are available for people who have an interest in the Minneapolis General Conference session?**

The 1888 General Conference session convened in the newly constructed Adventist church in

Minneapolis, Minnesota, from October 17 through November 4. A ministerial institute lasting from the tenth of October through the seventeenth preceded the formal conference session. The agenda contained two categories of items: business matters and theological concerns. While official action on the business items was restricted to the General Conference session, action and reaction on the theological issues flowed from the institute into the regular session as if they were one meeting.

Writing near the beginning of the institute, Smith listed the topics proposed for discussion as "A historical view of the ten kingdoms, The divinity of Christ, The healing of the deadly wound, Justification by faith, How far we should go in trying to use the wisdom of the serpent, and Predestination" (RH, Oct. 16, 1888).

Because of the intensity of debate over three of the topics, however, not all the proposed items were studied or presented at Minneapolis. Writing near the close of the meetings, Waggoner noted that the subjects considered had been the 10 kingdoms of Daniel 7, the Papacy and the proposed National Reform Government, and "the law and the gospel in their various relations, coming under the general head of justification by faith" (ST, Nov. 1, 1888).

Several contemporary records, some of which have only recently come to light, verify Waggoner's report of the topics discussed. Among those records that we have known for some time are the *General Conference Bulletin,* the items in the *Review* and *Signs,* Jones's sermons on religious liberty, the sermons of Ellen White, and the incoming and outgoing correspondence files of the Whites. Noticeably absent from the list of existing documents are Waggoner's sermons. They have probably permanently disappeared, despite claims to the contrary.

Two important sources of information, however, have recently joined the records of the 1888 General Conference meetings: the diary of R. Dewitt Hottel, which gives a day-by-day report of the topics covered, and the two notebooks that W. C. White took during the meetings. White's booklets are especially valuable, since he listed the Bible texts used in the studies.

In addition to the above contemporary sources, in 1987 the Ellen G. White Estate published four volumes entitled *The Ellen G. White 1888 Materials,* consisting of her correspondence and manuscripts relating to Minneapolis and the sermons she preached there. The next year the White Estate released a 591-page document, *Manuscripts and Memories of Minneapolis.* This collection contains a selection of letters from various participants regarding the 1888 meetings, copies of denominational and newspaper reports of the meetings, the 1888 *General Conference Bulletin,* selected periodical articles, the Hottel diary, and the two W. C. White notebooks. As valuable as it is, however, *Manuscripts and Memories* contains only a small percentage of the existing documents that throw light on the meetings. It does, however, reprint some of the most helpful.

## 11. What did the discussion of the 10 horns of Daniel 7 contribute to the meetings?

Not much in terms of substance, but the 10-horns controversy, coming early in the Minneapolis meetings, did generate a lot of heat that undoubtedly aggravated disagreements on other topics. As expected, the speakers on the 10 horns were Jones and Smith.

The divisiveness of the topic showed itself on October 15, when Smith, the champion of the traditionalists on the issue, considered it "evil" and "utterly unnecessary" even to deal with the subject. Such a course, he intimated, was the "tearing up of old truth" that "has stood the test 40 yrs." Why shouldn't any new interpretation endure the same test of time before its acceptance? "If we have diversity of testimony[,] why change[?]" Smith was not about to "sit calmly by and see [a] foundation stone taken out with ruthless hands" (WCW, NB #1, 27).

Jones, Smith's chief opponent on prophetic interpretation, was equally gentle. "Elder Smith," the younger man blurted out early in the meetings, "has told you he does not know anything about this matter. I do, and I don't want you to blame me for what he does not know." That was too much for Ellen White, who rebuked him, saying "Not so sharp, Brother Jones, not so sharp" (in ATR MS, Jan. 30, 1931; JSW interview by RJW and DKS, June 4, 1950).

According to the Minneapolis *Tribune* of October 18, some of Smith's friends sought to force a vote on the 10-horns issue, but E. J. Waggoner blocked that ploy, holding that the delegates should take no vote until they had thoroughly investigated the topic. "The matter was discussed in this manner," said the *Tribune,* "until it was high noon and time for adjournment."

Despite the stalemate, Smith claimed victory for his view in a *Review* editorial. "The sentiment of the delegates appeared, . . ." he pontificated, "to be overwhelmingly on the side of established principles of interpretation, and the old view." The editorial upset W. C. White, who noted that Smith neglected to report that the delegates had voted near the close of the discussion that "all should study the question faithfully during the year." White saw Smith's editorial procedure as deceptive. "I told our people in the presence of Eld. Smith that while it was right to demand of the Editors of the *Signs* that they be cautious, . . . it was also demanded of the Editors of the *Review* that they be honest, and I showed them how this report was calculated to mislead the people" (RH, Oct. 23, 1888; WCW to JHW, Feb. 27, 1889). It is needless to point out that such maneuvering did not contribute much to harmony between the various delegates.

## 12. What relationship did the law in the Galatians debate have to the presentations on righteousness by faith?

One of the interesting facts of the 1888 General Conference session is that even though the contending sides entered the meetings with the issue of the law in Galatians at the forefront of their minds, the main outcome of the meeting was a new emphasis on righteousness by faith. How this happened has been a mystery to many.

E. J. Waggoner should receive credit for the new direction on the topic. He made a strategic decision not merely to debate the issue of the law in Galatians, but to raise the larger issue of salvation in terms of law and gospel, and then to discuss the book of Galatians in that context.

Thus even though Waggoner made at least nine presentations on Gospel/law topics during the meetings, the first five or six centered on righteousness by faith. Only after that did he deal more specifically with Galatians.

Waggoner's strategic decision expanded the debate in a manner that would soon thrust issues specifically related to Galatians into the background for most people, while at the same time propelling to center stage issues tied to how people are saved. Thus we hear very little about the law in Galatians conflict after the 1888 meetings.

According to Waggoner's theology, the ten-commandment/ schoolmaster law brings us "unto Christ, *that we might be justified by faith*" (*Gospel in the Book of Galatians* 45). Ellen White, while not agreeing with all of his positions, backed him on that central point in the struggle. She told the delegates, "I see the beauty of truth in the presentation of the *righteousness of Christ in relation to the law* as the doctor has placed it before us. . . . [It] harmonizes perfectly with the light which God has been pleased to give me during all the years of my experience" (EGW MS 15, 1888; italics supplied). In that passage Ellen White highlighted what she considered to be one of Waggoner's most important contributions to Adventist theology. *He had built a bridge between law and gospel by making explicit the gospel function of the ten-commandment law (i.e., to lead individuals to Christ for forgiveness and justification).* Such a linkage, as we shall see in chapter 5, became central in her understanding of Revelation 14:12 as it related to her understanding of the message of 1888.

Butler, who had worked himself into a state of nervous exhaustion over his fears concerning the implications of the new theology being set forth by Waggoner and Jones, was unable to attend the General Conference session. In his place as champion of the traditional view on the law in Galatians was J. H. Morrison, president of the Iowa Conference and an expert debater. Morrison claimed that Adventists had always believed in justification by faith. He feared, however, that the subject had been "overstressed," and *he was afraid that the law might lose its important place in*

*Adventist theology.* Speaking after Waggoner, Morrison made at least seven presentations on topics related to Galatians during the meetings (R. T. Nash, "Eyewitness Report").

As in both 1886 on the Galatians issue and earlier at Minneapolis on the problem of the 10 horns, the Butler-Smith-Morrison faction sought to force a vote to establish the correct creedal position on the relationship of law and gospel. As Jones later put it: "At Minneapolis, in 1888, the General Conference 'administration' did its very best to have the denomination committed by a vote of the General Conference to the covenant of 'Obey and Live,' to righteousness by works" *(God's Everlasting Covenant* 31). The attempt failed, but it was not an idle jest when Ellen White stated at the close of the conference that "Willie and I have had to watch at every point lest there should be moves made, resolutions passed, that would prove detrimental to the future work" (EGW to MW, Nov. 4, 1888).

Needless to say, the issues raised by the law in Galatians controversy at Minneapolis were at least as divisive as the dissension over the 10 horns. In fact, the issues are still bones of contention more than a century after the event. Much of the rest of this book will focus on those contentions.

### 13. How did the impending national Sunday bill and religious liberty issues affect the 1888 meetings?

Unlike the battles over Galatians and the 10 horns of Daniel 7, religious liberty did not divide the Adventist leadership at Minneapolis. All agreed that the proposed amendment to the Constitution, advocating that the public schools teach Christianity, and the Blair national Sunday bill represented ominous signs in prophetic history—a vindication of the Adventist interpretation of Revelation 13 and 14 (see question 4). Given such events, the delegates did not contend A. T. Jones's sermons on religious liberty. On the other hand, Ellen White felt discouraged because his messages on the crisis never got as much serious consideration as they should have because of the animosity over the disputed issues (EGW MS 24, 1888).

In spite of foot-dragging by some, Jones's presentations, coupled with the realities facing the denomination, moved the delegates to action. Three of their most important decisions involved him. First, the denomination would publish his General Conference sermons on religious liberty. They came off the press, with some editing, in 1889 as *Civil Government and Religion, or Christianity and the American Constitution*. Second, Jones was to visit Boston, Chicago, and other places to lecture on the topic of religious liberty. And, third, he was to lead a delegation of three to testify before the United States Senate Committee on Education and Labor against the two Blair bills. Thus by the end of the Minneapolis conference Jones was well on his way to becoming a full-time religious liberty advocate—a position in which he would make some of his most important contributions to the Adventist Church.

## 14. What can be learned about authority for deciding biblical/theological issues from the Minneapolis session and its context?

The lessons on religious authority are some of the most instructive to flow out of the 1888 meetings. Those Adventists aligned with the Smith-Butler faction appealed to at least four forms of human authority in their attempt to settle the theological issues troubling the denomination.

### Appeals to human authority

The first centered on expert opinion, which both Smith and Butler attempted to use to settle the controverted points. In refuting Butler's use of expert opinion to decide the Galatians issue, Waggoner replied: "I care nothing for what a man says. I want to know what God says." Seventh-day Adventists, he argued, "should be Protestants indeed, testing everything by the Bible alone" (*Gospel in Galatians* 56, 60).

A second area of human authority centered on authoritative position. Butler, as president of the denomination, was particularly susceptible to that temptation. Mrs. White, on the other hand, opposed such thinking. Soon after the 1888 meetings she would write that Butler "thinks his position gives him such power that his voice is infallible" (EGW to MW, Nov. 4, 1888). Denigrating both administrative and expert human authority in doctrinal issues, Ellen White pointed out in December 1888 that "we should not consider that either Elder Butler or Elder Smith are the guardians of the doctrines for Seventh-day Adventists, and that no one may dare to express an idea that differs from theirs. *My cry has been: Investigate the Scriptures for yourselves. . . . No man is to be authority for us*" (EGW to WMH, Dec. 9, 1888; italics supplied).

A third invalid use of authority at Minneapolis concerned a reliance on Adventist tradition to settle a point. Both Smith and Butler had used the argument repeatedly that since the Adventist positions on Galatians and Daniel had stood as truth for 40 years, they should not be changed. Smith even went so far as to claim that if the tradition was wrong he would have to renounce Adventism.

E. J. Waggoner and A. T. Jones, of course, rejected the appeal to tradition. Ellen White was in the reformers' corner. "As a people," she warned, *"we are certainly in great danger, if we are not constantly guarded, of considering our ideas, because long cherished, to be Bible doctrines and on every point infallible, and measuring everyone by the rule of our interpretation of Bible truth. This is our danger, and this would be the greatest evil that could ever come to us as a people"* (EGW MS 37, c. 1890; italics supplied).

A final category of human authority employed by the Smith-Butler group in their attempt to maintain traditional Adventism was their drive for a voted creedlike statement that would set the pre-1888 theology in concrete. As we noted above, the Whites, along with Waggoner and Jones, successfully withstood all such attempts.

*Appeals to Ellen White's authority*

Beyond appeals to human authority, the Smith-Butler faction attempted to settle the theological and biblical issues at Minneapolis by calling on the authority of Ellen White. Butler was especially excited about the possibilities inherent in that line of action. Between June

20, 1886, and October 1, 1888, the General Conference president sent Mrs. White a series of increasingly more forceful letters urging her to settle the interpretative problem by providing a testimony on the correct interpretation of the law in Galatians. He started out gentle enough, but by October 1888 he openly threatened her. If she did not come up with the proper interpretation, he suggested, it will not only "open a wide door for other innovations to come in and break down our old positions of faith," but it "will tend to break the confidence of our people in the testimonies themselves. And this whole matter I believe will do more to break down confidence in your work than any thing which has occurred since this cause has had an existence, if this Pacific movement on the Galatians question is sustained. . . . If our people come to think that the other side is supported it will break the faith of many of our leading worker[s] in the testimonies. There is no other possible result." Without doubt Butler included himself in that category (GIB to EGW, Oct. 1, 1888).

The entire sequence of Butler's letters is of great interest, given the way many Adventists view the work of Ellen White. Many have both silently and verbally wished that she were still alive in our day so that they could ask her the "real" meaning of a particular scriptural passage. In the Butler sequence we find her answer to such an approach—silence, frustrating silence. She refused to play into the hands of the traditionalists who had practically demanded that she settle the Galatians issue by providing a final answer through either her "lost" testimony to J. H. Waggoner in the 1850s or by making an authoritative statement. In other words, they wanted her to function as a theological police officer or an exegetical referee. That, significantly enough, is exactly what she refused to do. As a result, she lost her credibility with many.

Not only did Ellen White decline to settle the biblical issue through appeal to the testimonies, but she went so far as to infer to the delegates at the Minneapolis meetings on October 24, 1888, that it was providential that she had lost the testimony to J. H. Waggoner in which she had purportedly resolved the issue once and for all in the 1850s. *"God has a purpose in this. He wants us to go to the Bible and get the Scripture evidence"* (EGW MS 9, 1888; italics supplied). In other words, she was more interested in what the Bible had to say on the subject than in what she had written. She did not want the testimonies to take the place of Bible study. Later she would emphasize that point again in early 1889 in the publication of *Testimony* 33, which has an entire section on that topic. Mrs. White made it explicit that her writings were to bring people "back to the word" and to aid them in understanding the biblical principles, but she never held them up as a divine commentary on scripture. That, of course, was not always obvious to her fellow Adventists (5T 663-668).

In the face of her unwillingness to "produce" a testimony on Galatians, the Minneapolis traditionalists must have felt a wave of thankfulness that they at least had her published writings on the topic, especially since she had seemingly identified the law in Galatians in her *Sketches From the Life of Paul* (1883). On October 24, J. H. Morrison utilized *Sketches* in his attempt to demonstrate the validity of the ceremonial law interpretation. Turning to page 193, he read to the delegates: "'He [Paul] describes the visit which he made to Jerusalem to secure a settlement of the very questions which are now agitating the churches of Galatia, as to whether the Gentiles should submit to circumcision and keep the ceremonial law.'" Next Morrison quoted from her discussion of the nature of the Galatians problem on page 188: "'Having gained this point, they [the Judaizing teachers] induced them [the Christians at Galatia] to return to the observance of the ceremonial law as essential to salvation. Faith in Christ, and obedience to the law of ten commandments, were regarded as of minor importance.'" The last statement appeared to accomplish two points at once—it apparently validated the ceremonial law interpretation, while explicitly discounting Waggoner's position in one fatal blow. Morrison then read from page 68, where Ellen White spoke of the yoke of bondage mentioned in both Acts 15:10 and Galatians 5:1: "'This yoke was not the law of ten commandments, as those who oppose the binding claim of the law assert; but Peter referred to the law of ceremonies, which was made null and void by the crucifixion of Christ'" (italics supplied; see also WCW, NB #1, 63, 67). Having submitted his evidence, Morrison and the traditionalists must have believed they had clinched the argument. After all, they had a quotation from Ellen White. The long and the short of it was that they were right and Waggoner was wrong on the basis of her commentary on the Bible.

That position, however, Ellen White refused to take at Minneapolis. That very morning (before Morrison's presentation) in addressing the Galatians issue, she had said: *"I cannot take my position on either side until I have studied the question"* (EGW MS 9, 1888; italics supplied). It was in that context that she noted that it was providential that she could not find her testimony to J. H. Waggoner on the topic. Some would have misused it to keep people from exploring God's Word. *Ellen White had light for the General Conference delegates on the subject of Galatians, but that light, as she repeatedly asserted, was that they needed to study the Bible and not rely on any other form of authority as they sought the meaning of Scripture.* She would stamp that message home in her last recorded sermon at Minneapolis—"A Call to a Deeper Study of the Word" (EGW MS 15, 1888). Apparently Morrison's use of *Sketches* to prove his point did not impress her. We have no indication that she considered the matter settled by that method, nor did she quote her own writings at Minneapolis to decide any of the theological, historical, or biblical issues. Her writings had their purposes, but one of them was apparently not to take a superior position to the Bible by providing an infallible commentary.

Waggoner, Jones, and the Whites stood in harmony with each other on the proper use of authority in resolving theological issues. All held that the Bible was the only determiner of Christian belief. As a result, they were united against the attempts of the old guard to utilize anything else to settle biblical disputes.

*Appeals to biblical authority*
Ellen White was particularly insistent on the need for Bible

study in dealing with theological controversies. On April 5, 1887, for example, she wrote to Butler and Smith that "we want Bible evidence for every point we advance. We do not want to tide over points, as Elder Canright has done, with assertions." On July 17, 1888, she set forth her position with the greatest clarity when she published in the *Review* that "the Bible is the only rule of faith and doctrine."

Again, on August 5 she wrote to those soon to meet in Minneapolis that they should "search the Scriptures carefully to see what is truth. The truth can lose nothing by close investigation. Let the Word of God speak for itself, let it be its own interpreter. . . . The Bible must be our standard for every doctrine."

Mrs. White was adamant during the conference and in its aftermath that both sides of the argument in the Galatians controversy needed to be submitted to the searching scrutiny of exacting Bible study. On December 9, 1888, she asked a crucial question to the initiator of the California conspiracy rumor: "If every idea we have entertained in doctrines is truth will not the truth bear to be investigated? Will it totter and fall if criticized? If so," she answered, "let it fall, the sooner the better. The spirit that would close the door to investigation of points of truth in a Christlike manner is not the Spirit from above." Two days later she wrote to Butler that "the Bible, the Bible alone, laid up in the heart and blessed by the Spirit of God, can make man right and keep him right."

### 15. What was the "spirit of Minneapolis," and how did that attitude affect the reception of Jones, Waggoner, and Ellen White?

Ellen White "discerned at the very commencement of the meeting [at Minneapolis] a spirit which burdened" her, an attitude that she had never seen previously among her fellow leaders and ministers. It bothered her that it was "so unlike the spirit of Jesus, so contrary to the spirit that should be exercised toward each other" (EGW MS 24, 1888). She would come to think of that hostility as the spirit of Minneapolis or the spirit of the Pharisees.

W. C. White had also recognized the problem. Writing three weeks after the close of the Minneapolis session, he noted that the meetings had included some things "not very pleasant to write about. Certain influences had been working for some time which culminated at this meeting in the manifestation of a spirit of phariseeism [see questions 9 and 16]. So mother named it." An understanding of the spirit of Minneapolis is essential if we are to grasp the dynamics of the 1888 meetings and subsequent Adventist history (WCW to OAO, Nov. 27, 1888).

A composite description of the spirit of Minneapolis, as Mrs. White portrayed it, would have the following characteristics among others. First, sarcasm and jesting toward the denomination's reform element. Some, for example, referred to Waggoner as "Sister White's pet." Second, criticism dominated the spirit of Minneapolis. Third, those infected with it exhibited envy, evil surmisings, hatred, and jealousy. Fourth, it prompted "sharp, hard feelings" and attitudes. Fifth, its possessors were "intoxicated with the spirit of resistance" to the voice of the Holy Spirit. Sixth, the spirit of Minneapolis drove those having it to speak in a manner calculated to inflame one another regarding those who held opposing doctrinal views. Seventh, it bred contention and doctrinal debate in place of the spirit of Jesus. As Mrs. White put it, the spirit of Minneapolis stirred up "human passions" and "bitterness of spirit, because some of their brethren had ventured to entertain some ideas contrary to the ideas that some others . . . had entertained, which were thought . . . to be inroads upon ancient doctrines." Eighth, it generated an attitude that led to "playing upon words" and "quibbling upon words" in doctrinal discussions. In short, the spirit manifested at Minneapolis "was uncourteous, ungentlemanly, and not Christlike" (see GRK, *Angry Saints,* 81, 82).

One of the most noteworthy things about the attitude pervading Minneapolis is that it resulted from a desire to protect Adventism's old doctrinal "landmarks," particularly the exaggerated ideas related to the importance of the traditional views of Galatians. Ellen White deplored the fact that "a difference in the application of some few scriptural passages makes men forget their religious principles." When she saw the methods and hostility of the traditionalists in their defense of Galatians, Mrs. White "for the first time" began to suspect that they had an incorrect view, "for the truth required no such a spirit to sustain it." "God deliver me from your ideas . . . ," she declared to the traditionalists, "if the receiving of these ideas would make me so unchristian in my spirit, words, and works" as they had become (EGW to Children, May 12, 1889; EGW MSS 24, 1888; 13, 1889; 30, 1889; 55, 1890).

*One of the great tragedies of Minneapolis was that in seeking to protect Adventism's doctrinal purity and its traditional scriptural interpretations, the Battle Creek leadership had lost its Christianity.* Like the Pharisees of Christ's time, they had been more interested in maintaining traditional views than they were in discovering the full truth or in behaving in a Christian manner when dealing with problems in the church.

That unchristlike spirit directed itself not only at Jones and Waggoner but also at Ellen White because of her support for them and their teachings. The October 21 Minneapolis *Tribune* might report that "Mrs. White is a sort of prophetess, and everything she says is listened to by the Seventh Day [sic] Adventists with awe," but she knew better. She recognized that something had changed in the response of her listeners. To her daughter-in-law she commented that her testimony "has made the least impression upon many minds than at any period before in my history" (EGW to MW, Nov. 4, 1888). To another she wrote: "My testimony was ignored, and never in my life . . . was I treated as at that conference" (EGW to WMH, Dec. 9, 1888).

Accused of having changed her theology on the Galatians issue, and having been openly doubted in her denials of any involvement in a conspiracy with Jones, Waggoner, and her son, Mrs. White had reached the nadir of her influence (EGW MS 24, 1888). It is no wonder that she would always look back on the 1888 General Conference session with feelings of dismay. She had seen its promise, but she had experienced its failure.

## 16. How did the so-called "California conspiracy" fuel the "spirit of Minneapolis" and its dynamic of rejection?

As intimated in question 9, a great deal of the intensity and pervasiveness of the spirit of Minneapolis with its ill will toward Jones, Waggoner, and Ellen White had stemmed from a letter sent by William H. Healey (a pastor in California) to George I. Butler in late September that suggested that the Western leaders of the church had developed a scheme to change the denomination's theology (WCW to DTJ, Apr. 8, 1890; EGW to WMH, Dec. 9, 1888; WMH to EGW, [Sept. 1901]).

Before the arrival of Healey's letter, Butler appears to have been emotionally stable. He didn't like the thought of the controverted points on Daniel and Galatians coming up, but the August letters of W. C. and Ellen White had convinced him of the necessity of permitting it. However, it devastated the already tense General Conference president when he received what appeared to him to be concrete news of an organized conspiracy just a few days before the opening of the Minneapolis session. Suddenly the events of the past two years all seemed to make sense to him. The reason the Whites had pushed so hard to get a hearing for Jones and Waggoner's new theology was that they were all in it together. Certainly, Butler reasoned, here was a conspiracy of the most dangerous type and a threat to Adventism's time-tested beliefs.

That reasoning led Butler into a spurt of frenzied activity. He not only ordered a reprinting of his *Law in the Book of Galatians,* but he organized his forces to resist the Western coalition and fired off a series of telegrams and letters to the delegates, warning them of the conspiracy and urging them to "stand by the old landmarks." Beyond that, he wrote a more than 40-page letter to Ellen White on October 1 in which he blamed her for his broken health and put the finger on W. C. White as the mastermind behind the plot. By the end of the first couple days of the meetings the knowledge of the supposed conspiracy had spread throughout the ranks of the Smith-Butler supporters (ATJ to CEH, May 12, 1921; EGW MS 15, 1888).

Meanwhile, the Whites, Waggoner, Jones, and the other California delegates remained ignorant of the fact that the Battle Creek forces viewed them as conspirators. As W. C. White put it, he was "innocent as a goose" about the problem "while my old friends at B[attle] C[reek] . . . were saying the bitterest things against me" (WCW to DTJ, Apr. 8, 1890). Their unawareness of the suspicions of their Eastern colleagues led the Westerners to play into the hand of the conspiracy theory, since they felt no need to be cautious in their statements or even make explanations. The upshot was the spirit of Minneapolis and the widespread animosity to Jones, Waggoner, and the Whites.

But the disaster at Minneapolis was not the end of the message of Christ's righteousness that Jones, Waggoner, and Ellen White had begun to preach at the 1888 General Conference session. They left Minneapolis to begin a campaign to take Christ, His love, and His righteousness to the Adventist Church (see question 43).

# CHAPTER 4

# ELLEN WHITE'S ENDORSEMENT OF JONES AND WAGGONER AND HER CRUCIAL PLACE IN UNDERSTANDING THE 1888 MESSAGE

Before we examine the nature of the 1888 message in Chapter 5, it is of the utmost importance to ponder the significance of Mrs. White's endorsement of Jones and Waggoner and their message to the church.

**17. Why is Ellen White so important in understanding the meaning of 1888 for Adventist history and theology?**

It is safe to say that without Ellen White's comments on the topics, the 1888 General Conference session, the 1888 message, and the teachings of Jones and Waggoner would be nonissues in Adventism. Without her repeated endorsement of Jones and Waggoner during the late 1880s they would never have received a hearing in 1888 or achieved responsible positions of influence in the church during the 1890s.

Another area of Ellen White's importance has to do with our need to discover the nature of the 1888 message. Since the precise words of Waggoner and Jones on righteousness by faith at the Minneapolis meetings have seemingly vanished, and since the proponents of *all* theological positions related to 1888 rely heavily on the endorsement of Waggoner and Jones by Ellen White, it is important to examine what she approved of in their presentations. *The best way to understand what she perceived to be the essence of their teachings is by examining what she had to say about their message and about those who opposed it. This approach to grasping the core of the 1888 message is much safer than reading back into their 1888 sermons things that they subsequently preached,* especially since Jones and Waggoner's theology went through a significant transformation between 1888 and 1896.

In conclusion, it cannot be overemphasized that *all parties attribute special value to Jones and Waggoner's 1888 teachings because of Ellen White's endorsement of them. Thus it is of utmost importance for us to seek to determine just what it was in their message that she approved.*

## 18. Did Ellen White have the 1888 message herself, or did she merely point to the messengers?

Some Adventist interpreters of the 1888 message argue that Ellen White was not the 1888 messenger, but only pointed to the messengers. We need to examine the validity of that assertion, since an incorrect understanding of it opens the gates to erroneous thinking on the topic.

It is quite true that Mrs. White repeatedly pointed out that "the Lord in His great mercy sent a most precious message to His people through Elders Waggoner and Jones" (TM 91). Thus she was definitely a pointer.

But, and this is an item of utmost importance, she was far more than that. In fact, she became one of the most prolific writers on 1888 topics herself. The 1888 message literally transformed her writing ministry. After the Minneapolis conference she released a constant stream of books on Christ and the plan of salvation. Thus we have *Steps to Christ* in 1892, *Thoughts From the Mount of Blessing* in 1896, *The Desire of Ages* in 1898, *Christ's Object Lessons* in 1900, and the Christ-centered opening chapters of *The Ministry of Healing* in 1905. Ellen White's great theme after 1888 became

Christ and His righteousness. That was evident not only in her books but also in hundreds of articles and countless sermons and letters. It's not that she changed her position on such topics in 1888, but that she greatly increased her emphasis on them after she saw the need of Adventism for a better understanding of Christ and salvation during 1888 and the 1890s.

Now, I suppose that one could argue that Ellen White didn't have the 1888 message in the 1890s but only directed the church's attention to the messengers, but that would imply that she didn't learn much from the experience or that she had some reason for "hiding" or "camouflaging" the 1888 message.

It seems that such a line of logic is wrongheaded. To the contrary, *it is much more logical to reason that she grasped the message and did everything in her power to put it before the Adventist people in her books, articles, letters, and sermons. As a result, it is reasonable to conclude that we can find the 1888 message in Ellen White's writings.* Thus we should read such books as *Steps to Christ* and *The Desire of Ages* to see what she emphasized. *Beyond that, her writings can serve as a screen to determine what she approved of in the writings and preaching of Jones and Waggoner, since she repeatedly asserted that she didn't agree with all of their teachings.*

The alternative is to take hold of the writings of Jones and Waggoner in their entirety, abstract their theology, and then plug Ellen White quotations and Bible verses into their theology to give it support. That course of action seems to be exactly what a large sector of Adventism with an interest in the 1888 message seems to be doing (see questions 26 and 56). Unfortunately, such proponents overlook the fact that Jones and Waggoner, even in their post-1888 years, were not correct in all of their theological understandings. We will return to that topic later in this chapter (question 22), but first we need to look at a couple of other vital issues.

## 19. Is it true that Ellen White gave Jones and Waggoner one of the strongest endorsements of her entire career?

*Definitely! Undoubtedly the strongest!* One student of the topic has counted some 121 distinct passages (some of them containing multiple approvals) about them and their message. What he fails to tell us is that many of those commendations come from the same documents. Thus, for example, his first 48 samples represent only 20 documents. In other words, when Ellen White is talking on the topic she tends to repeat herself to make her point of emphasis. As a result, the number of letters and manuscripts containing commendations of Jones and Waggoner is much fewer than 121.

That fact, however, should not lead us astray. The truth is that even after we account for number inflation, what Jones and Waggoner presented in 1888 still has more Ellen White commendations for it than any other message during her prophetic career. We need to take that fact seriously.

Let's take a look at a few of her commendations. In May 1895 she referred to them as "the men whom God has commissioned to bear a special message to the world" (TM 79), in October 1888 she described them as "men divinely appointed" to present "precious gems of truth, appropriate for our time" (EGW MS 8a, 1888), and in 1892 she affirmed that "God had sent these young men . . . to bear a special message" (EGW to US, Sept. 19, 1892).

She leaves us with no doubt as to the fact that Jones and Waggoner had a message desperately needed by the Seventh-day Adventist Church. In fact, on May 1, 1895, she went so far as to say that "if you reject Christ's delegated messengers, you reject Christ." *That's a strong statement,* you may be thinking. What did she mean? The context explains it in terms of rejecting their gospel preaching. "Neglect this great salvation," she continued, "kept before you for years [since 1888], despise this glorious offer of justification through the blood of Christ and sanctification through the cleansing power of the Holy Spirit, and there remaineth no more sacrifice for sins, but a certain fearful looking for of judgment and fiery indignation." She went on to urge those still resisting the gospel message of Jones and Waggoner to humble themselves and confess their sins that they might have forgiveness, pardon, and a new life (TM 97, 98).

*The bottom line is that Jones and Waggoner had a message that Adventists needed. It was a "most precious" message* (TM 91). *Thus it is crucial that we understand as clearly as possible the nature of what Jones and Waggoner preached in 1888, especially that part of their message that Ellen White commended in no uncertain terms.*

## 20. Did Mrs. White endorse other ministers in a way that would lead us to believe that God led them and that they had a special message for His people?

Yes, but never as often as for Jones and Waggoner. Three names come to mind. The first is Martin Luther, the great sixteenth-century reformer. "Angels of heaven were by his side as he studied the Bible," she penned of him, "and rays of light from the throne of God revealed the treasures of truth to his understanding" (GC 122). Thus Ellen White had no doubt that God had used Luther and that angels guided him in his general work. On the other hand, it would be an error to infer that she agreed with all of his theology just because he had been sent of God and guided by angels.

A similar case is that of William Miller. Ellen White wrote of him that "God sent His angel to move upon the heart of a farmer who had not believed the Bible, to lead him to search the prophecies. Angels of God repeatedly visited that chosen one, to guide his mind and open to his understanding prophecies which had ever been dark to God's people" (EW 229). Such words while implying Ellen White's prophetic endorsement of Miller's general understanding must not be interpreted to mean that she believed he was correct in all things. For example, she most certainly differed with Miller on the identity of the sanctuary to be cleansed at the end of the 2300 days.

A third individual, interestingly enough, was Uriah Smith, Jones and Waggoner's opponent in the issues and struggles related to Minneapolis. W. C. White pointed out that some Adventist ministers gave "equal importance to the quotations of Scripture, and to Eld. Smith's comments." That was largely because of Ellen White's commendation of his *Daniel and the Revelation*. When the book underwent revision for translation in 1887, W. C. White recalled, "they brought forward what had been written by her endorsing the work of Elder Smith, and [the] teaching that he had the help of heavenly angels in his work; and these things were enlarged upon, until the president of the Publishing Association practically took the position that 'Thoughts on Daniel and the Revelation' was inspired, and ought not to be changed in any way. This, of course, made a candid and fair study of the questions under consideration almost impossible." White hoped in February 1889 that the "infallibility doctrine" regarding Smith would soon dissipate (WCW to CE, May 14, 1887; WCW to SNH, Dec. 9, 1909; WCW to JHW, Feb. 27, 1889).

It should be needless to say to the readers of the present book that Ellen White certainly disagreed with Smith on a variety of topics even though she held a high view of his work on the prophecies.

Mrs. White's endorsements of such writers as Luther, Miller, and Smith were not essentially different from those she gave to Waggoner and Jones, except in frequency. The same parallelism is evident in the fact that she never approved of everything in the writings of Jones and Waggoner any more than she did in the works of such "divinely guided" preachers as Luther, Miller, and Smith. It is to those issues that we now turn in questions 21 and 22.

### 21. Why did Ellen White so frequently go out of her way to endorse Jones and Waggoner?

First and foremost, because the Adventist Church needed to hear and accept their gospel message. As we will see in Chapter V, Adventists had the law, but they didn't understand the centrality of Jesus, their sin-pardoning Saviour, to their Christian experience. They needed Jesus, His grace, and His love, not only in their theology but in their lives. Like Paul, Ellen White never tired of uplifting Jesus as the sinner's only hope. She was excited that God had used Jones and Waggoner to give renewed emphasis to Christianity's central teaching.

A second reason Ellen White repeatedly trumpeted Jones and

Waggoner's message is that in 1888 those who opposed them were the "who's who" of the Adventist leadership. And even though important changes in top leadership occurred during late 1888, significant resistance toward the men and their message remained among certain key Adventists and many pastors and people throughout the 1890s (see question 50). Given the conditions, Ellen White had to "shout" loudly, firmly, and repeatedly as she attempted to get Adventists to listen to Jones and Waggoner's special Christ-centered message. Without her insistent and influential urging, their message could have died on the vine. Even with her support it had a difficult time of it.

## 22. Did Ellen White's enthusiastic support mean that she approved of everything Jones and Waggoner taught?

No, but this is an important question, since for the better part of a decade she drove home the idea that God had chosen them as special messengers because "many had lost sight of Jesus" and "justification through faith" in Him. God had raised up the two men, she claimed, because many Adventists "needed to have their eyes directed to His divine person" and His love (TM 91, 92).

Because of Ellen White's endorsement, some interpreters have acted as if she gave Jones and Waggoner a kind of blank check in theological matters—especially in relation to issues involving righteousness by faith. That, however, had never been her intent, and such an approach fails to line up with the historical record.

Early in the Minneapolis meetings, for example, Ellen White wrote of her angelic "guide" who "stretched out his arms toward Dr. Waggoner and to you, Elder Butler, and said in substance as follows: 'Neither have all the light upon the law; neither position is perfect'" (EGW to GIB, Oct. 14, 1888). While the context of that statement is the 1886 General Conference session, she still held the same position in 1888. In early November she told the delegates at Minneapolis that some things that Waggoner had presented on the law in Galatians "do not harmonize with the understanding I have had of this subject." Later in the same talk she claimed that "some interpretations of Scripture given by Dr. Waggoner I do not regard as correct" (EGW MS 15, 1888).

W. C. White substantiates his mother's position. He wrote to his wife from Minneapolis that "much that Dr. W. teaches is in line with what" his mother had "seen in vision." That had led some to jump to the conclusion "that she endorses all his views, an[d that no] part of his teaching disagrees wi[th Mother] and with her Testimonies. . . . I could prove all this to be f[alse]" (WCW to MW, Oct. 27, 1888).

Ellen White never indicated on what points she disagreed with Waggoner, but we do know that during the late 1880s and early 1890s he and Jones promoted several teachings out of harmony with her views. The following items represent only a *sample* of those differences:

1. In *Christ and His Righteousness* (1890) Waggoner taught that "there was a time when Christ proceeded forth and came from God . . . , but that time was so far back in the days of eternity that to finite comprehension it is practically without beginning" (pp. 21, 22). In short, Christ's existence derived from the Father; He was not like God in terms of infinite existence. Mrs. White took the opposite position. She penned, "In Christ is life, original, un-borrowed, underived" (DA 530).

2. On January 21, 1889, Waggoner argued in the *Signs* that "Christ could not sin" because He was God incarnate. Ellen White, by way of contrast, took the opposite position. For her Christ faced infinite risk in the incarnation because sin was a genuine possibility. In her thinking Jesus was quite "capable of yielding to temptation" (EGW MS 57, 1890).

3. At the 1893 General Conference session Jones argued, on the basis that the fourth commandment advocates six days of work and one of rest, that to stop work on Sunday because the civil law commands it is to "put Satan above Christ." Such a course of civil disobedience as he urged, he pointed out in positive anticipation, would bring about the death decree (1893 GCB, 125, 126). Ellen White, however, vigorously objected to his determined stand.

Writing in response to tensions created by Jones's position, she declared that "refraining from work on Sunday is not receiving the mark of the beast." She counseled him, "Never encourage the spirit of defiance and resistance" (EGW MS 22a, 1895; EGW to ATJ, Nov. 21, 1895).

4. Ellen White wrote in 1894 that "Elder Waggoner has entertained ideas, and without waiting to bring his ideas before a counsel of brethren, has agitated strange theories. He has brought before some of the people ideas in regard to organization that ought never to have had expression" (EGW to ATJ, Jan. 14, 1894).

5. In 1893 she had to rebuke Jones for claiming that "there were no conditions" in salvation. To her way of thinking "the Bible is full of conditions" (EGW to ATJ, Apr. 9, 1893; see also question 33).

6. During 1893 and 1894 Jones put forth Anna Rice as a new Adventist prophet, whereas Mrs. White flatly pointed out that she had "not had the least confidence" in Anna's claims, "or the claims anyone has made in her behalf" (EGW to Brother and Sister Rice, Nov. 1, 1893; see also questions 40, 46, 47).

7. Concerning the human nature of Christ, in 1887 Waggoner wrote that "if Christ had not been made *in all ways* like unto his brethren, then his sinless life would be no encouragement to us" (*Gospel in Galatians* 61), and in 1890 he penned "that the flesh which He assumed had all the weaknesses and sinful tendencies to which fallen human nature is subject." The proof for that latter assertion, Waggoner argued, "is shown by the statement that He 'was made of the seed of David *according to the flesh.'* David had all the passions of human nature. He says of himself, 'Behold, I was shapen in iniquity; and in sin did my mother conceive me.' Ps. 51:5" (*Christ and His Righteousness* 26, 27). During the same era Jones argued that "Christ's nature is precisely our nature." "In his human nature there is not a particle of difference between him and you" (1895 GCB 231, 233). Once again Ellen White took a different track. "He is a brother in our infirmities," she wrote, "but not in possessing like passions" (2T 202). Furthermore, she penned that "it is not correct to say, as many writers have said, that Christ was like all children. . . . No one

. . . could say that Christ was just like other children" (YI, Sept. 8, 1898). Finally she cautioned one minister in the 1890s: "Be exceedingly careful how you dwell upon the human nature of Christ. . . . Not for one moment was there in Him an evil propensity. . . . Never, in any way, leave the slightest impression upon human minds that a taint of, or inclination to corruption rested upon Christ" (EGW to Brother and Sister Baker, [Feb. 9, 1896]; for more on the differences between Jones and Waggoner and Ellen White on the human nature of Christ, see questions 52 and 53).

We could extend the list of items on which Ellen White differed with Jones and Waggoner, but the point has been made. She had serious disagreements with some of their assertions, even in areas related to salvation.

But that does not mean that they didn't have a message that the Adventist Church desperately needed to hear. *What we need to do is not to ferret out the various aspects of their theology as if everything they said was pure truth, but to examine what Ellen White repeatedly approved of in their message. That procedure will bring to light significant variations between what many with an interest in the 1888 message highlight and what Ellen White actually approved of in the message of Jones and Waggoner (see, for example, questions 50, 51, 53, 54, 55, 56, 18, 23, 25, 26, 28, 33, 40, and 46).*

We must never forget that even though she repeatedly validated the central core of Jones and Waggoner's 1888 message on the righteousness of Christ, she never held them to be above theological error. In February 1890 she faced that very issue with those assembled for an in-service ministers' school. "I believe," she told them, "without a doubt that God has given precious truth at the right time to Brother Jones and Brother Waggoner. Do I place them as infallible? Do I say that they will not make a statement or have an idea that cannot be questioned or that cannot be error? Do I say so? No, I do not say any such thing. Nor do I say that of any man in the world. But I do say God has sent light, and do be careful how you treat it. We want the truth as it is in Jesus" (EGW MS 56, 1890).

That is good advice. Seventh-day Adventists certainly should want above all things "the truth as it is in Jesus."

## 23. According to Ellen White, can too much attention be paid to the teachings of Jones and Waggoner?

The answer to that question is both yes and no. Certainly we can't go wrong as we let them direct us to the *Bible's teaching* on the "uplifted Saviour" and the "gospel of His grace" (TM 91, 92).

On the other hand, because of Ellen White's repeated endorsement of Jones and Waggoner, by the early 1890s many people had begun treating Jones and Waggoner's pronouncements as if they possessed divine authority. We can clearly see that in the case of Anna Rice, who felt called to the prophetic office in 1892. Presumably Anna would have sought counsel with Ellen White, but the latter was in Australia. The next best thing, Anna reasoned, would be an endorsement from Jones. After all, hadn't Mrs. White said that he and Waggoner had advanced light? So Anna traveled from Salt Lake City to Chicago to visit Jones. If he said she was a prophet, then she must be one, since he had Mrs. White's approval. To Anna's joy Jones sanctioned her messages (SNH to EGW, Jan. 4, 189[3]; for additional information on the Anna Rice crisis, see questions 40, 46, and 47).

Thus by late 1892 some were treating Jones as a kind of prophetic extension of Ellen White. People were beginning to validate truth by his words.

By 1894 S. N. Haskell had begun complaining to Mrs. White that he realized that she had had to endorse Jones and Waggoner in the years right after 1888 because so many of the denominational leaders had been against them, but now "the whole country had been silenced against criticizing them to any extent." He claimed that many now regarded Jones as "almost inspired of God" (SNH to EGW, Apr. 22, 1894).

Ellen White replied to Haskell that while she was in general agreement with Jones's work, she could not approve of his mistakes. She warned the Battle Creek church that they were "placing the servant where God should be. The Lord has given Brother Jones a message to prepare a people to stand in the day of God; but when the people shall look to Elder Jones instead of to God, they will become weak instead of strong" (EGW to SNH, June 1, 1894; EGW to Brethren and Sisters, Mar. 16, 1894; for more on elevating Jones and Waggoner to where God and the Bible should be, see questions 26 and 56).

To Jones she wrote that she trembled "because the people were looking to you, and hanging upon your words and were not doing as they should have done—they were not catching the precious rays of light that shone from the Word of God" (EGW to ATJ, June 7, 1894). Again she penned, "Many are so weak in faith and experience that they will look to A. T. Jones, and what you say and do, they will say and do; for they will not look beyond you to Jesus, who is the Author and Finisher of our faith" (EGW to ATJ, Apr. 14, 1894).

That is needed advice. We can indeed focus too much on Jones and Waggoner, even on those theological points on which they were correct. God has used them to point Adventism back to the Bible and salvation in Jesus, but we go wrong when we dwell on them and their particular formulation of the Adventist message (see question 25). We need to look beyond them to Jesus and the word of God that they did so much to uplift at Minneapolis.

### 24. What aspect of Jones and Waggoner's theology did Mrs. White so emphatically endorse?

This is a most important question. It is so vital that the next chapter will be largely devoted to the topic. But for a preview at this point it might be helpful to review the answer to question 1 in the first chapter.

### 25. Did Ellen White hold that it was essential that Seventh-day Adventists have knowledge of the *particular approach* of Jones and Waggoner to Seventh-day Adventist theology?

*The answer to this question is a definite no, since in several in-*

*stances she emphatically claimed that the Lord could have come before 1888* (see, e.g., EGW MS 4, 1883; 4SP 291, 292). *Thus the Second Coming could have taken place before the 1888 messengers had even begun to preach their theological package.* That idea has astounding consequences for those who would make too much of Jones and Waggoner's theology in 1888, 1893, or 1895. Christ could have returned before 1888. For that reason it is not helpful to build too much on the basis of their distinctive theology. It is not the particular interpretation that they placed upon the gospel that is all-important, but the gospel itself.

### 26. What is the most serious mistake that can be made in evaluating Ellen White's endorsement of Jones and Waggoner?

It is dangerous to read Ellen White in a one-sided manner that grasps all the commendations she applies to Jones and Waggoner while overlooking her cautions and emphases (see questions 22, 1, 30, and 37). This has led some with a burden for the 1888 message in the late twentieth century to do their Bible reading basically through the eyes of Jones and Waggoner and to get their basic theology from them on the ground of Ellen White's endorsements. Then after having obtained their theological structure from the 1888 messengers, they begin to plug in Bible texts and Ellen White quotations to prove their points. Unfortunately, this procedure leads them to adopt both the 1888 messengers' helpful ideas and those that may be erroneous (see question 56 for more on this point). In the meantime, their theology has shifted from a biblical perspective to a Jones and Waggoner perspective. The Bible and Ellen White's writings become tools to fill out the theology of the 1888 messengers. In the process, the doing of 1888 theology moves away from the very foundation that led Ellen White to be excited about it in the first place; it abandons its biblical base. *We must never forget that the Bible is the basis of all theological thinking* and that we must test the ideas of all other writers by God's Word (see question 14).

In this chapter we have examined the crucial role of Ellen

White in understanding the 1888 message and the nature and extent of her endorsement of Jones and Waggoner. In Chapter V we will, among other things, take a look at what exactly she endorsed in the writings of Jones and Waggoner.

# CHAPTER 5

# THE MEANING OF THE 1888 MESSAGE.

## PART 1: THE CENTRAL CORE OF THE MESSAGE

With this chapter we have come to the heart of this book. All previous chapters have been leading up to it, while those that follow flow out of it. Here we deal with the theological contribution that stands at the core of the message of 1888.

**27. What was the greatest need of the Seventh-day Adventist Church in the 1880s?**

To Ellen White the answer to that question was quite clear. "A revival of true godliness among us," she penned in 1887, "is the greatest and most urgent of all our needs. To seek this should be our first work." But, she noted, many Adventists were not prepared to receive God's blessing, and many needed to be converted. She indicated, "We have far more to fear from within [the church] than from without." On the other hand, "there is nothing that Satan fears so much as that the people of God shall clear the way by removing every hinderance, so that the Lord can pour out His Spirit upon a languishing church and an impenitent congregation" (RH, Mar. 22, 1887).

81

By the late 1880s Ellen White had become deeply concerned over the condition of Adventism. Too many leaders and members had a theory of the truth, but were failing to grasp the Truth itself. That idea escalated in her thinking throughout the 1880s and would come to a climax in late 1888.

But the burden was not new to her writing. In 1879 she wrote that "it would be well to spend a thoughtful hour each day reviewing the life of Christ from the manger to Calvary. We should take it point by point and let the imagination vividly grasp each scene, especially the closing ones of His earthly life. By thus contemplating His teachings and sufferings, and the infinite sacrifice made by Him for the redemption of the race, we may strengthen our faith, quicken our love, and become more deeply imbued with the spirit which sustained our Saviour. If we would be saved at last we must all learn the lesson of penitence and faith at the foot of the cross." She went on to say that *she longed "to see our ministers dwell more upon the cross of Christ"* (4T 374, 375; italics supplied).

The same emphasis rang true at the 1883 General Conference session, where Mrs. White told the assembled ministers that "we must learn in the school of Christ. *Nothing but His righteousness can entitle us to one of the blessings of the covenant of grace.* We have long desired and tried to obtain these blessings, but have not received them because we have cherished the idea that we could do something to make ourselves worthy of them. We have not looked away from ourselves, believing that Jesus is a living Saviour. We must not think that our own grace and merits will save us; the grace of Christ is our only hope of salvation" (1SM 351; italics supplied).

Again, she penned on the eve of the Minneapolis meetings, "there are subjects that are sadly neglected, that should be largely dwelt upon. The burden of our message should be the mission and life of Jesus Christ. . . . Show to your hearers Jesus. . . . He died for man. . . . O that the haughty hearts of men might realize this! O that they might enter into the meaning of redemption, and seek to learn the meekness and lowliness of Jesus" (RH, Sept. 11, 1888).

Ellen White was clear on the greatest lack of Adventism and

its ministry as the 1888 General Conference session approached. They needed Jesus, His love, and salvation in Him. They must put away their self-righteousness and hard-heartedness.

### 28. Is it true, as some have claimed, that the 1888 message of righteousness by faith is a unique Adventist message?

One influential book on 1888 topics specifically points out that the message of Jones and Waggoner had a "unique spiritual nutriment" of righteousness by faith that was unavailable to previous reformers and that "righteousness by faith since 1844 . . . is greater than what the Reformers taught." "There was," our authors claim, "a distinct difference in" Ellen White's "mind between the message of righteousness by faith as presented in 1888 and the 'past message' the Lord sent prior to 1888" (RJW and DKS, *1888 Reexamined,* rev. ed., 53, [viii], 57, 52, [vii]).

How well, we might ask, does that viewpoint match up to that of Ellen White and E. J. Waggoner? Waggoner certainly didn't agree with such assertions. For example, he makes quite a point of his theological continuity with the great Reformers in the conclusion to his *Gospel in the Book of Galatians.* He had that book distributed to the delegates at the Minneapolis meetings, and it must have been fairly close to what he presented there on the relationship of law and gospel that so impressed Ellen White. *"I do not,"* he stated, *"regard this view which I hold as a new idea at all.* It is not a new theory of doctrine. Everything that I have taught is perfectly in harmony with the fundamental principles of truth which have been held not only by our people, but by all the eminent reformers." *To accept his view on the relation of law and gospel in Galatians,* Waggoner held, *"would simply be a step nearer the faith of the great Reformers from the days of Paul to the days of Luther and Wesley. It would be a step closer to the heart of the Third Angel's Message"* (p. 70; italics supplied).

One might object that Waggoner's treatment in his book on Galatians is too narrow in scope—that it did not hit the essence of his teachings on righteousness by faith. Thus it is important to note that in 1891 in his concluding study on Romans (the biblical book par excellence on righteousness by faith) Waggoner makes his claim even more emphatic. If there was any occasion on which he had an opportunity to demonstrate the uniqueness of his view on the topic, it was in the 16 studies on Romans that he presented at the 1891 General Conference session.

It is of the utmost importance to recognize that Waggoner's concluding study related his view on righteousness by faith to the three angels' messages of Revelation 14:6-12. *"Perhaps,"* he pointed out near the beginning, *"some have not realized the fact that the lessons we have been studying . . . on the book of Romans, have been nothing but the third angel's message."* He desired to demonstrate that Paul summed up the third angel's message in 1 Corinthians 2:2: "For I determined not to know any thing among you, save Jesus Christ, and him crucified." *Waggoner went on to ask his audience if Seventh-day Adventist preaching on the third angel's message should "embrace anything more"* than what Paul had. *"If it does,"* he answered, *"then whatever it may be, we had better get rid of it as soon as we can."*

After that excellent advice, Waggoner demonstrated that the third angel's message included nothing not already contained in the first angel's. Thus "the third is all in the first—the everlasting gospel. . . . That everlasting gospel, remember, is all summed up in one thing—Jesus Christ and him crucified, and of course risen again. We have nothing else in this world to proclaim to the people." He then spent the bulk of his study demonstrating how that everlasting gospel relates to distinctive Adventist truths, such as the law, the Sabbath, the state of the dead, and the punishment of the wicked (1891 GCB 238-246; italics supplied).

Waggoner saw his own message, therefore, as adding nothing to that of Paul, Luther, and Wesley. He did not regard it as something new or unique, but as being in the great stream of the preaching of the everlasting gospel—the common property of history's great Christian Reformers. It was to that everlasting gospel that he felt compelled to relate the distinctive teachings of Adventism. Thus his approach to Adventist theology provided a new framework that included both the everlasting gospel and the distinctive Adventist truths in proper relationship.

Ellen White was in harmony with Waggoner on his message's lack of uniqueness. On October 21, 1888, she told the assembled delegates: "The Lord desires us all to be learners in the school of Christ. . . . God is presenting to the minds of men divinely appointed [Jones and Waggoner] precious gems of truth, appropriate for our time. *God has rescued these truths from the companionship of error, and has placed them in their proper framework.* . . . Brethren, God has most precious light for His people. *I call it not new light; but O, it is strangely new to many.* Jesus said to His disciples, 'A new commandment I give unto you, That ye love one another; as I have loved you.' This was really an old commandment, which had been given in the Old Testament scriptures, but it *had been lost*" (EGW MS 8a, 1888; italics supplied).

The implication is plain that Seventh-day Adventists through Jones and Waggoner had recovered old truth in 1888. They had not only found it again, but "rescued" it "from the companionship of error" and placed it within its "proper framework."

In early November Ellen White would speak to the delegates on the same issue. "You know," she declared, "that precious light has shone forth in connection with the law of God, as the righteousness of Christ has been presented with that law. Dr. Waggoner has opened to you precious light, *not new, but old light which has been lost sight of by many minds,* and is now shining forth in clear rays" (EGW MS 15, 1888; italics supplied).

About a month after the Minneapolis meetings she again reflected on the topic. "Elder E. J. Waggoner," she wrote, "had the privilege granted him of speaking plainly and presenting his views upon *justification by faith and the righteousness of Christ in relation to the law. This was no new light, but it was old light placed where it should be in the third angel's message*" (EGW MS 24, 1888; italics supplied).

The fact that the message of righteousness by faith that Jones and Waggoner preached was not new was a topic Ellen White would verify repeatedly as she endeavored to stem the anxiety of

Smith, Butler, and their colleagues who feared that the two young men from the West Coast had developed some heretical ideas to pervert Adventism. She repeatedly expressed shock that so many Adventist leaders found it to be a strange doctrine. To her the message of 1888 was *"not a new truth, but the very same that Paul taught, that Christ Himself taught"* (EGW MS 27, 1889; italics supplied).

The only way one can claim that the 1888 perspective on righteousness by faith is somehow unique to Adventism is to deny totally the plain words of E. J. Waggoner and Ellen White. Whatever the message was, Paul, Luther, and Wesley shared and preached it. (For more on this topic see question 37.)

## 29. Isn't it true that all Seventh-day Adventists believed in righteousness by faith before the 1888 General Conference session?

Yes, that is a true statement. But as we shall see in this section, two very distinct theories existed as to the meaning of righteousness by faith. The one held by Butler, Smith, and their friends was quite different from the view set forth by Waggoner and Jones in 1888.

Perhaps the best way to approach the subject is through Uriah Smith's *Review* editorials in January 1888. In a January 3 piece entitled "The Main Point," Smith asserted that the aim of the Adventist pioneers was to herald the last proclamation of the Second Advent and *"to lead souls to Christ through obedience* to this closing testing truth. This was the *one objective* point of all their efforts; and the end sought was not considered gained unless souls were converted to God, and led to seek through an *enlightened obedience to all his commandments, a preparation for the Lord from heaven."* Smith tied "The Main Point" to both the Sunday law movement and to the third angel's message. He therefore underscored *"keep"* when he quoted Revelation 14:12: "'Here are they that *keep* the commandments of God and the faith of Jesus.'" Obedient keeping of all the commandments was central to his view of Adventism. In fact, a person came to Jesus through obedience (RH, Jan. 3, 1888; italics supplied).

That same emphasis appears in Smith's last editorial of January 1888—"Conditions of Everlasting Life." He based his comments on the question of the rich young ruler to Christ: "'Good Master, what good thing shall I do, that I may have eternal life?'" The Bible answer, Smith proclaimed, could be summed up in one proposition as "'Repent, believe, *obey, and live.'"* That, he claimed, was Jesus' response. After all, didn't He say to the young ruler, *"'If thou wilt enter into life, keep the commandments'"*?

Smith was right on target when he noted that no one could enter heaven "unless his righteousness exceeds that of the scribes and Pharisees." But he shot wide of the mark by suggesting that we could obtain the needed "excess of righteousness" by being even more zealous than the Jews of old in "keeping, and teaching others to keep, the commandments." "The trouble with the righteousness of the Pharisees," he suggested, "was that they had not reached an acceptable degree of "moral character" in their relation to the "moral law." While Smith briefly indicated that works cannot be the "ground of our justification," he spent the bulk of his editorial on his "main point"—on the "test" of obedience to the Ten Commandments, which "shall determine our fitness to enter heaven" (RH, Jan. 31, 1888; italics supplied).

Smith and his colleagues believed in justification by faith, but it was a justification built on the King James Version's misleading translation of Romans 3:25, which claimed Christ's "righteousness for the remission of sins that are *past.*" Thus J. F. Ballenger could write: "To make satisfaction for past sins, faith is *everything.* Precious indeed is that blood that blots out all our sins, and makes a clean record of the past. Faith only can make the promises of God our own. But present duty is ours to perform. . . . Obey the voice of God and live, or disobey and die" (RH, Oct. 20, 1891).

One result of their belief that justification by faith was for past sins was that Smith, Butler, and their friends taught that maintaining justification after conversion was a matter of "justification by works." After all, Ballenger later commented in quoting James, "'was not Abraham our father *justified by works* . . . ?'" "God speaks to us," Ballenger continued, "through his law and the testimony of Jesus, and when we obey, that act coupled with our faith, secures our justification." He believed the same was true of sanctification. It is *ours* to achieve—with Christ's help, of course. Such faith that leads to obedience, Ballenger concluded, will result in "the pouring out of the latter rain, drops of which seem to be already falling" (RH, Nov. 24, 1891). *Obedience was the key word of the Adventist traditionalists. Obey and Live was their motto.*

E. J. Waggoner, coeditor of the *Signs of the Times* with A. T. Jones, took distinct exception to Smith's January 1888 editorials and to the theology behind them. In February he replied to Smith in a piece entitled "Different Kinds of Righteousness." Waggoner held that a person could not improve on the moral righteousness of the scribes and Pharisees because "they trusted to their own works, and did not submit to the righteousness of God." In fact, he asserted, their righteousness was not "real righteousness at all." They had simply tried "to cover one filthy, ragged garment by putting on some more filthy rags." Instead of making themselves better, therefore, they were in a "worse plight." That was so, he claimed, because "'whatsoever is not of faith is sin.'" Aiming his dart specifically at the traditional Adventist view of justification and sanctification, he pointed out that "human righteousness is of no more worth *after* a man is justified than it was *before.*" The justified Christian "'shall live by faith.'. . . 'For Christ is the end of the law for righteousness to everyone that believeth.'" Therefore, "the one who has the most faith will live the most upright life." That is true because Christ is "'THE LORD OUR RIGHTEOUSNESS.'" If the key word for the traditionalists was "obedience," it was "faith" for Waggoner (ST, Feb. 24, 1888).

The contrast between the two theologies is also clear in Waggoner's presentations at the 1891 General Conference session as he pointedly assaulted the position of old guard Adventism. "Is it the spirit of Christ," he queried, "that works in us when we say that we are going to overcome if Christ will give us a little assistance? When we say," he replied, "that . . . we are going to have heaven by our own work, in part at least; we deny Christ." Such a theology is of "the spirit that leads a man into a monastery, and scourges the flesh, and does penance." It is "simply the logical outcome of the thought that *we* must do something to free ourselves from sin. It is the spirit that teaches that we cannot trust all to Christ, and let him work out our own righteousness for us." Waggoner concluded that "everything that is not totally subject to Christ, is actuated by the spirit of antichrist" (1891 GCB 245).

A. T. Jones stood solidly with Waggoner in his theology. For example, in May 1889 at the Ottawa, Kansas, camp meeting Jones told his hearers that the law was not the place to seek for righteousness. All "our righteousness is as *filthy rags.*" He went on to suggest that "the more righteousness of the law a man has the worse he is off—the more ragged he is." Salvation—both justification and sanctification—is totally by faith (Topeka *Daily Capital,* May 14, 1889).

Such sentiments did not go unheard and unanswered. On June 11, 1889, Smith fired off a broadside at Jones in the *Review* entitled "Our Righteousness." He noted that some of the correspondents of the *Review* were playing into the hands of those who would do away with the law by making remarks on our righteousness being "filthy rags." Smith went on to say that "perfect obedience to [the law] will develop perfect righteousness, and that is the only way any one can attain to righteousness." "We are not," he asserted, "to rest on the stool of do-nothing, as a mass of inertia in the hands of the Redeemer. . . . 'Our righteousness' . . . comes from being in harmony with the law of God. . . . And 'our righteousness' cannot in this case be filthy rags." There exists, he concluded, a righteousness that is "to be secured by doing and teaching the commandments" (RH, June 11, 1889).

Smith's article inspired Mrs. White to jump into the fray in a sermon on June 17 at the Rome, New York, camp meeting. Faith must come before works, she asserted in backing up Jones's position at Ottawa. " 'Well,' you say, 'What does Brother Smith's piece in the *Review* mean?' He doesn't know what he is talking about; he sees trees as men walking." She pointed out that just because Jesus and His righteousness are central in our salvation, that does not mean that we are discarding God's law. To Smith she wrote that he was on a path that would shortly bring him to the brink of a precipice, that he was "walking like a blind man," and that he had placed Jones in a false position (EGW MS 5, 1889; EGW to US, June 14, 1889).

Butler also jumped into the battle by publishing a *Review* article with a title quite expressive of his viewpoint: "The Righteousness of the Law Fulfilled by Us." "There is a sentiment prevailing almost everywhere," he thundered, that is pleasant but dangerous: "'Only believe in Christ, and you are all right.' . . . Jesus does it all." That teaching, he proclaimed, "is one of the most dangerous heresies in the world." The whole point of the third angel's message, he emphasized, is "the necessity of obedience to the law of God. 'Here are they that *keep the commandments of God,* and the faith of Jesus.'" The Christian world was rapidly losing that truth, and Adventists needed to uphold it (RH, May 14, 1889).

The distinction between the two Adventist camps also appears in the differences between Waggoner's and Butler's books on Galatians. Butler spoke of the "much-vaunted doctrine of justification by faith" (p. 78), while the younger man concluded "that it is *impossible to overestimate the doctrine of justification by faith"* (p. 71). It was no accident that Butler entitled his book *The Law in the Book of Galatians,* while Waggoner called his *The Gospel in the Book of Galatians.* The two titles reflected two approaches to Adventist theology.

In summary, it should be plain that all Seventh-day Adventists had a belief in some sort of justification by faith. On the other hand, vast differences existed between the various views—particularly the way their proponents constantly and consistently expressed then in print throughout the 1880s and early 1890s. The Smith-Butler forces believed in justification for past sins, but emphasized the law and obedience for Christian living. Jones and Waggoner put the stress on faith in Christ as the Christian's all in all. *The older men focused on the old covenant message of "obey and live," while Jones and*

*Waggoner preached the new covenant concept of the life of faith. What was at stake in the Adventist struggle was no less than the nature of how people are saved.*

### 30. What was Ellen White's understanding of the central meaning of the 1888 message?

We noted in question 17 that Ellen White's perspective of the significance of the 1888 message is important because *all* parties attribute special importance to the 1888 message because of Ellen White's multiple endorsements of Jones and Waggoner. It is thus of utmost concern to discover just what she saw as the central core of their presentation. That will guide us in seeing what she approved of in the theology of the 1888 messengers.

Perhaps, as we saw in question 1, the most explicit and comprehensive explanation of what she endorsed in the message of Jones and Waggoner appears in *Testimonies to Ministers*. In 1895 she wrote to O. A. Olsen that "the Lord in His great mercy sent a *most precious message* to His people through Elders Waggoner and Jones. This message was to bring more prominently before the world *the uplifted Saviour*, the sacrifice for the sins of the whole world. It presented *justification through faith* in the Surety; it invited the people to receive the *righteousness of Christ,* which is *made manifest in obedience to all the commandments* of God. *Many had lost sight of Jesus.* They needed to have their eyes directed to *His divine person, His merits, and His changeless love* for the human family. All power is given into His hands, that He may dispense rich gifts unto men, *imparting the priceless gift of His own righteousness to the helpless human agent. This is the message that God commanded to be given to the world. It is the third angel's message,* which is to be proclaimed with a loud voice. . . .

". . . The message of the gospel of His grace was to be given to the church in clear and distinct lines, *that the world should no longer say Seventh-day Adventists talk the law, the law, but do not teach or believe Christ*" (TM 91, 92; italics supplied).

Also insightful as to her view of the central element of the 1888 message is her diary entry on February 27, 1891. She noted, in an obvious reference to the Smith-Butler faction, that some feared that the church was "carrying the subject of justification by faith altogether too far, and of not dwelling enough on the law." Then she complained that many Adventist ministers presented their "subjects in an argumentative way and scarcely mention . . . the saving power of the Redeemer." *They and their messages were "destitute of the saving blood of Jesus Christ."* "Of all professed Christians, Seventh-day Adventists should be foremost in uplifting Christ before the world." Adventists should preach both the law and the gospel—"blended, [they] will convict of sin." *"God's law,"* she asserted (as she did when supporting Waggoner at Minneapolis), *"while condemning sin, points to the gospel. . . . In no discourse are they to be divorced."* Too many Adventists had not seen that "Jesus Christ is the glory of the law."

She went on to emphasize her central concern with both the 1888 message and the Adventist Church. "Why, then," she queried, "is there manifested in the church so great a lack of love, of true, elevated, sanctified, ennobling sympathy, of tender pity and loving forbearance? It is because Christ is not constantly brought before the people. His attributes of character are not brought into the practical life. . . . A correct theory of the truth may be presented, and yet there may not be manifested the warmth of affection that the God of truth requires. . . . The religion of many is very much like an icicle—freezingly cold. . . . They cannot touch the hearts of others, because their own hearts are not surcharged with the blessed love that flows from the heart of Christ. There are others who speak of religion as a matter of the will. They dwell upon stern duty as if it were a master ruling with a scepter of iron— a master stern, inflexible, all-powerful, devoid of the sweet, melting love and tender compassion of Christ."

In short, Adventists had been suffering from a Christless religion, and they needed the love of Jesus in their minds and hearts.

Mrs. White concluded her diary remarks with a disclaimer to the position that a theological understanding of righteousness by faith is all-important. "Many commit the error of trying to define minutely the fine points of distinction between justification and sanctification. Into the definitions of these two terms they often bring their own ideas and speculations. *Why try to be more minute than is Inspiration on the vital question of righteousness by faith? Why try to work out every minute point, as if the salvation of the soul depended upon all having exactly your understanding of this matter?* All can not see in the same line of vision." Jesus and His pardoning grace, she noted, are the Christian's only hope in life. "The blessing comes because of pardon; pardon comes through faith that the sin, confessed and repented of, is borne by the great Sin-bearer" (EGW MS 21, 1891; italics supplied).

Mrs. White's emphasis in both of the lengthy passages just cited was on the message of 1888 as basic Christianity rather than on some esoteric or distinctively Adventist approach to life and/or theology. That same perspective appears in her sermons at Minneapolis. *"My burden during the meeting,"* she wrote, *"was to present Jesus and His love* before my brethren, for I saw marked evidences that many had not the spirit of Christ" (EGW MS 24, 1888; italics supplied). In her October 11 keynote address she told the delegates that "we want less of self and more of Jesus." "If we put away all self-exaltation, all self-righteousness, and come into living connection with God, the righteousness of God will be imputed to us" (EGW MS 6, 1888). A week later she pleaded for the conversion of the Adventist ministry to Christ. And on October 24, in a posture of self-defense regarding her purported linkage with the California leaders in their alleged conspiracy to overturn the denomination's traditional theology, she cried out: "We want the truth as it is in Jesus. . . . I have seen that *precious souls who would have embraced the truth have been turned away from it because of the manner in which the truth has been handled, because Jesus was not in it. And this is what I have been pleading with you for all the time—we want Jesus. . . . All the object I had was that the light should be gathered up, and let the Saviour come in"* (EGW MS 9, 1888; italics supplied).

Rather than merely being interested in justification by faith at

Minneapolis, Ellen White was also concerned with sanctification by faith. Unlike some of her twentieth-century interpreters, she did not define the righteousness of Christ in a way that separated justification and sanctification. She was not interested in those topics that fascinate professional and lay theologians. Rather her burden was that people find Jesus and be saved from sin in the fullest sense of the word. Thus at Minneapolis she could talk of Jesus as both our "substitute" and our "pattern." Ellen White indicated that Christ, in His role as sanctifier, has provided power "sufficient to enable us to reach the high standard of Christian perfection." While Christ is ministering in the sanctuary above, individuals are to be cleansed " 'from all filthiness of the flesh and spirit, perfecting holiness in the fear of God.' " The empowering role of the Holy Spirit for Christian living would become one of her major themes in the 1890s. The gospel for her included both justifying and sanctifying grace. Her burden was not "the fine points of distinction between justification and sanctification," but the role of Jesus Christ in the full salvation of lost sinners. It was a message of God's love and human helplessness (EGW MSS 8a, 1888; 8, 1888; 21, 1891).

In the battle of her contemporaries over the emphasis on obedience to the law versus faith, Ellen White held for proper balance. To her the law was important, but only in the context of faith and grace. That, of course, was in essence the position of Jones and Waggoner during the 1888 period. Thus Mrs. White found herself aligned against the forces of traditional Adventism in the late 1880s and early 1890s. At a meeting in early 1890 in which she vocally deplored Smith's voluntary absence, she pleaded with the assembled ministers to go from their convocation so full of the message of Christ's righteousness that they could not hold their peace. If they did, however, she told them that "men will say, 'You are too excited; you are making too much of this matter, and you do not think enough of the law; now, you must think more of the law; don't be all the time reaching for this righteousness of Christ, but build up the law.' "

To such "good" Adventist sentiments she replied, *"Let the law*

*take care of itself. We have been at work on the law until we get as dry*
*as the hills of Gilboa. . . . Let us trust in the merits of Jesus. . . .* May
God help us that our eyes may be anointed with eyesalve, that we
may see" (EGW MSS 36, 1890; 10, 1890; italics supplied).

The items of crucial importance to Ellen White in the 1888
message had to do with the centrality of Jesus as Saviour and the
need of faith in His merits. *She supported Waggoner and Jones be-*
*cause they were uplifting these neglected aspects of Christianity in an*
*Adventism that had come to rely too much on the law and on its own*
*ability to do right. Above all things she saw that the Adventist Church*
*needed Jesus and His saving righteousness.*

We will return to Ellen White's emphasis on those topics in the
next chapter when we examine the relation of righteousness by
faith to the message of the third angel (see especially question 37).
At this point in the present chapter we will look a little more closely
at Waggoner's teachings on righteousness by faith.

### 31. How did Waggoner view the process of salvation?

The first thing that we should note in Waggoner's theology is
that human beings can do nothing to earn salvation. "Our salvation
is wholly due to the infinite mercy of God through the merits of
Christ" (ST, July 17, 1884). Yet, in spite of human sinfulness, God
"does not wait for sinners to desire pardon, before he makes an effort to save them" (ST, Jan. 27, 1888). That is good news indeed,
but it is a gospel quite at variance with Uriah Smith, who preached
that obedience led men and women to God. To the contrary, according to Waggoner, the God of grace searches out the undeserv-
ing lost. God takes the initiative in salvation.

A second pillar in Waggoner's theology of salvation is that no
person can become good by obeying the law, because "the law has
not a particle of righteousness to bestow upon any man." Waggoner
held that "a man cannot do good until he first becomes good.
Therefore, deeds done by a sinful person have no effect whatever to
make him righteous, but, on the contrary, coming from an evil
heart, they are evil, and so add to the sum of his sinfulness." Yet, he

noted, "the Pharisees are not extinct; there are many in these days who expect to gain righteousness by their own good deeds" *(Christ and His Righteousness* 55, 57). That, of course, was impossible.

As Waggoner saw it, God never gave the law as an avenue by which to achieve heaven. Both Waggoner and Jones believed that the first function of the law was not only "to give the knowledge of sin," but "to bring people to Christ, that they may be justified by faith" (RH, June 20, 1899; *Gospel in Galatians* 46, 47).

"Since the best efforts of a sinful man," claimed Waggoner, "have not the least effect toward producing righteousness, it is evident that the only way it can come to him is as a gift." Our own attempts at attaining righteousness are like trying to cover our naked bodies with "filthy garments." But "we find that when Christ covers us with the robe of His own righteousness, He does not furnish a cloak for sin, but takes the sin away." In effect, when we accept Christ's righteousness, our "sin has been canceled" *(Christ and His Righteousness* 60, 65, 66).

At the point where an individual accepts Christ's righteousness by faith, Waggoner asserted, that person becomes a part of the family of God. "Note," he penned, "that it is by being justified by His Grace that we are made heirs. . . . Faith in Christ Jesus makes us children of God; therefore we know that whoever has been justified by God's grace,—has been forgiven,—is a child and an heir of God" *(ibid.* 68).

But justification and adoption into the family of God are not the sum total of salvation for Waggoner. Far from it, "God does not adopt us as His children because we are good, but in order that He may make us good" *(ibid.* 69).

At the very time that individuals are justified and adopted into the family of God they are also transformed into new creatures *(ibid.).* Such persons are not only no longer under condemnation, but they "are now new creatures in Christ and must henceforth walk in newness of life, no longer 'under the law,' but 'under grace.'" At the time of justification God gives the converted sinner "a new heart." Thus "it is proper to say that he is saved" (ST, May 25, 1888).

ELLET J. WAGGONER:

JONES'S "BLOOD

BROTHER IN THE

'BLOOD OF THE

EVERLASTING

COVENANT' "

URIAH SMITH: JONES'S

PERPETUAL ADVERSARY IN

THE AREA OF PROPHETIC

INTERPRETATION

THE LAW

IN THE

BOOK OF GALATIANS:

IS IT

THE MORAL LAW,

OR DOES IT REFER TO

THAT SYSTEM OF LAWS PECULIARLY JEWISH?

BY ELD. G. I. BUTLER.

BATTLE CREEK, MICH.:
REVIEW & HERALD PUBLISHING HOUSE.
1886.

The Gospel
IN THE
Book of
Galatians

A Review
by
E J. Waggoner

OAKLAND, CAL.
1888

BUTLER AND WAGGONER

CARRIED ON A HEATED DEBATE

OVER THE NATURE OF THE LAW

THROUGH THESE TWO BOOKS

1888 GENERAL CONFERENCE SESSION IN MINNEAPOLIS—IN FRONT

OF MINNEAPOLIS SDA CHURCH

G. I. BUTLER: PRESIDENT OF

THE GENERAL CONFERENCE,

1871-1874, 1880-1888

A. T. JONES:

A POWERFUL LEADER,

PREACHER, AND WRITER,

A.T. JONES BECAME A

MAJOR INFLUENCE IN

ADVENTISM BEFORE

TURNING AGAINST

THE CHURCH

NB - See OT on Jonah + God's care for his prophets, msgrs.

Here it is important to note that Waggoner often talked of justification by faith and the new birth in the same breath. That is quite appropriate, since they take place at the same moment. In other words, at the very point in time a person is justified, he or she is also born anew of the Holy Spirit. Thus both being accounted righteous (being justified) and having one's nature changed happen simultaneously. As a result, being accounted righteous, according to Waggoner, is not a legal fiction. We should note that he often runs being counted righteous and being born anew together under the heading of justification as he discusses the beginning of the Christian experience, while other writers, in talking of that beginning, verbally differentiate between the two aspects of the simultaneous experience by labeling them justification and new birth.

In Waggoner's words "the difference between a righteous man and a sinner is much more than a mere difference of belief. It is more than a mere arbitrary reckoning on the part of God. It is a real difference. . . . God never declares a person righteous simply because he makes an acknowledgement of the truth. There is an actual, literal change from a state of sin to righteousness, which justifies God in making the declaration" (PT, Aug. 16, 1894). *conversion*

For Waggoner, justification, new birth, and adoption were the beginning of the Christian walk. He stood over against the holiness teachers who held to a form of sanctification "without any change of habit on the part of the individual." He viewed "holiness" without life-changing obedience to the law to be a "delusion" (ST, May 8, 1884).

The saved person, according to Waggoner, will live the life of God's law. He wrote, "A person can no more love God and fail to manifest it by deeds, than he can live without breathing" (*Honor Due to God* 4). Victory over sin comes from the indwelling power of the Holy Spirit in a Christian's life. Only those who gain the victory over sin will be in the eternal kingdom (*ibid.* 48).

## 32. How did Waggoner's view of salvation relate to the covenants? *— Old Covenant —*

The terms of the old covenant were "obey and live," the very theology set forth by Smith, Butler, and much of the pre-1888 Adventist community. Those who obeyed would have eternal life (see question 29).

Waggoner stood that equation on its head. First, he claimed, came justification and life in Christ, and only then obedience. The crucial problem with the old covenant, Waggoner pointed out, was that it made "no provision for forgiveness of sins" (ST, June 22, 1888). But the new covenant had righteousness by faith in Jesus at its very center. It was a covenant of grace in which born-again Christians have the law of God in their hearts. "Walking in the law" will be a natural way of life for those who have been born into the family of God and have the indwelling law in their inner being (*Gospel in Galatians* 46, 47).

Ellen White and Waggoner were in essential harmony on the covenants. Her treatment of the two covenants, penned in the late 1880s, provides a nice summary of their view on the topic. "The terms of the 'old covenant,'" she writes, "were, Obey and live. . . . The 'new covenant' was established upon 'better promises'—the promise of forgiveness of sins and of the grace of God to renew the heart and bring it into harmony with the principles of God's law. 'This shall be the covenant that I will make with the house of Israel; After those days, saith the Lord, *I will put my law* in their inward parts, *and write it in their hearts.* . . . I will *forgive* their iniquity, and I will remember their sin no more.' Jeremiah 31:33, 34.

"The same law that was engraved upon the tables of stone is written by the Holy Spirit upon the tables of the heart. Instead of going about to establish our own righteousness we accept the righteousness of Christ. His blood atones for our sins. His obedience is accepted for us. Then the heart renewed by the Holy Spirit will bring forth 'the fruits of the Spirit.' Through the grace of Christ we shall live in obedience to the law of God written upon our hearts. Having the Spirit of Christ, we shall walk even as He walked" (PP 372).

It was that very concept of the covenant that so many old-line Adventists, with their focus on obedience, found threatening. Waggoner's emphasis on faith in Christ undermined their law-oriented theology, even though, as we have seen, Waggoner, Jones, and Ellen White had a prominent place for the law and obedience in their theology. But for them obedience flowed out of a saving relationship to Jesus rather than leading to such a relationship.

## 33. Does salvation have conditions?

Several of the foremost writers on topics related to the 1888 message claim that salvation has "no conditions." Thus Jack Sequeira writes that "I believe" the Bible teaches "that God actually and unconditionally saved all humanity at the cross so that we are justified and reconciled to God by that act. . . . I believe that the only reason anyone will be lost is because he or she willfully and persistently rejects God's gift of salvation "in Christ" (Beyond Belief 8). Robert J. Wieland and Donald K. Short set forth essentially the same argument in their 1888 Re-examined. "Christ's sacrifice," they argue, "is not merely provisional but effective for the whole world, so that the only reason anybody can be lost is that he has chosen to resist the saving grace of God" (rev. ed., [vi]).

Their position, interestingly enough, contradicts not only the Bible but also Waggoner and Ellen White. While the Bible and Waggoner and Mrs. White all agree (1) that Christ died for every person on the cross, (2) that God's sustaining grace has preserved the human race since the Fall so that Adam and Eve did not die the very day they sinned, and (3) that the God who seeks out lost sinners and sent His Son to die for a sinful race (Gen. 3:8-13; Luke 15:4, 8, 20, 28; 19:10; John 3:16) initiates every step in salvation, they do not hold that salvation is unconditional or that the only way that one can be lost is to "willfully and persistently" reject "God's gift of salvation in Christ."

To the contrary, the Bible plainly states that salvation comes as a faith response (to God's accomplished sacrifice and forgiveness in Christ (John 1:12; 3:16; Eph. 2:8; 1 John 1:9). That is why Scripture calls God's plan of salvation "righteousness by faith" rather than "righteousness by birth unless you consciously reject God's plan." We accept God's offer by faith. Faith is the necessary

99

*condition. The focus in the Bible is on accepting God's offer rather than on not rejecting it.*

Ellen White is quite in harmony with the necessity of faith as a condition in the salvation process. *"The only way in which [a sinner] can attain to righteousness,"* she penned, *"is through faith. By faith he can bring to God the merits of Christ, and the Lord places the obedience of His Son to the sinner's account. Christ's righteousness is accepted in place of man's failure, and God receives, pardons, justifies, the repentant, believing soul, treats him as though he were righteous, and loves him as He loves His Son. This is how faith is accounted righteousness; and the pardoned soul goes on from grace to grace, from light to a greater light"* (1SM 367; italics supplied).

She couldn't have said it more plainly. There is a condition to salvation—faith in the Christ who died for all people on the cross.

We should note again that Waggoner held to the same conditional approach to salvation as Ellen White and the Bible. He had no doubt that "it is by being justified by His grace that we are made heirs." He further pointed out that "this justification by his grace is *through faith* in Christ." It is "faith in Christ Jesus" that "makes us children of God" *(Christ and His Righteousness* 68).

Far from being born into the family of God and a state of justification, human beings have both only on condition of faith. The doctrine that God "unconditionally saved all humanity at the cross" and the only way to be lost is to "willfully and persistently" reject "God's gift of salvation in Christ" is foreign to Ellen White, Waggoner, and the Bible. They put the emphasis on receiving the gift. John puts it nicely when he writes: "For God so loved the world that he gave his only Son, that whoever *believes* in him should not perish but have eternal life" (John 3:16, RSV).

## 34. What is the relationship between correct theology and Christian love?

Without doubt Ellen White had a profound interest in the correct understanding of the Bible and Christian doctrine. Yet, on the other hand, she was even more concerned that Bible study and doctrinal discussion take place in the context of Christian love. Back in 1887, when she saw the cruel spirit of Minneapolis on the horizon, she had written that "there is danger of our ministers dwelling too much on doctrines, . . . when their own soul needs practical godliness" (EGW to EJW and ATJ, Feb. 18, 1887).

Again, in early 1890, D. T. Jones (secretary of the General Conference) wrote to W. C. White that "your mother and Dr. Waggoner both say that the points of doctrine are not the matters at issue at all, but it is the spirit shown by our people in opposition to these questions which they object to. I am perfectly free to acknowledge that the spirit has not been the Spirit of Christ. It has not been so in my case, and I think I can discern enough to be safe in saying that it has not been so in the case of others. I have often thought over the matter and wondered why it was that such unimportant matters, practically, should cause such a disturbance, such a division, and such a state of feeling as has existed for the last year and a half. . . . The point in your mother's mind and in the mind of Dr. Waggoner, was not to bring in these questions and force them upon all, but to bring in the doctrine of justification by faith and the Spirit of Christ, and try to get the people converted to God" (DTJ to WCW, Mar. 18, 1890).

There were things even more important than correct doctrine in Ellen White's eyes. Doctrines and a right understanding of the Bible were vital, but not all important. Thus she noted in relation to the discussion over the law in Galatians that if the doctrines of some produced such an unchristlike spirit in them, "my prayer is that I may be as far from your understanding and interpretation of the Scriptures as it is possible for me to be" (1888 Materials 632).

We need to make sure that in seeking to protect Adventism's biblical understanding we don't lose our Christianity. If one should ever have to face a choice between love and being doctrinally correct, the more important option is love. Of course, it is possible to have both. God's ideal for us is that we always enter doctrinal and biblical discussion in the spirit of Christian love. When we lose that spirit, we know that we have stepped outside of Christ, even though we may be technically correct.

# THE MEANING OF THE 1888 MESSAGE. PART 2: THE RELATIONSHIP OF THE 1888 TEACHINGS TO THE THIRD ANGEL'S MESSAGE, THE LATTER RAIN, AND THE LOUD CRY

In Chapter 5 we noted that Ellen White held the core of the 1888 message to be an emphasis on Jesus and salvation by faith in His saving merits. In this chapter we will examine the relationship of that emphasis to the third angel's message, the latter rain, and the loud cry. But before undertaking that task we need to review the central place of the messages of the three angels of Revelation 14 to Seventh-day Adventist theology.

### 35. How does Seventh-day Adventism relate to the messages of the three angels of Revelation 14?

The messages of the three angels have stood at the very center of Seventh-day Adventist self-understanding. These three messages, according to Revelation 14, are the last warnings to go to a perishing world before the second advent of Jesus. The first message (verses 6, 7) is a commission to preach both the everlasting gospel and a judgment-hour message "to every nation, and kindred, and tongue, and people." Adventists have seen the beginning of the spread of this message in the preaching of William Miller in the 1830s and 1840s. They regarded the second angel's message of verse 8 (the fall of Babylon as the popular churches both rejected Bible truth and persecuted God's people for preaching it) as also beginning in the 1840s.

Seventh-day Adventists have not only viewed themselves as a called-out people to continue the preaching of the first two warning messages, but as a special people to preach the third angel's message of verses 9-12. Those verses contrast those who will eventually have the mark of the beast with those who keep the commandments of God. "Here," we read in verse 12, "is the patience of the saints: here are they that keep the commandments of God, and the faith of Jesus." When read in combination with Revelation 12:17 ("And the dragon was wroth with the woman, and went to make war with the remnant of her seed, which keep the commandments of God"), Revelation 14:12 emphasizes that God will have a last-day people who will obey all of His commandments, including the fourth, which stipulates worshiping on the seventh day.

Adventists have taught that the fourth commandment (the only one in contention in the nineteenth century) would become a focal point of controversy in the last great struggle between those who remain faithful to God and His principles and other people as men and women opt for either the mark of the beast or faithfulness to God. Such an understanding led early Adventists to a sensitivity to Sunday legislation and a conviction that they were God's called-out people to preach the third angel's message.

Thus they came to think of themselves as the people of the third angel with a unique mission to fulfill before the great second-coming harvest of Revelation 14:14-20. In fact, Revelation 14:12 became the central text in Adventism. The masthead of the *Review and Herald* quoted it in full for nearly a century. Recognizing the implications of the claims implied in the Adventists' application of that text to their denomination, a reporter for the Minneapolis *Journal* pointed out that "it is either monstrous egotism or sublime faith which leads them to apply this text to themselves" (Oct. 22, 1888). Adventists, for their part, undoubtedly considered it "sublime faith." But no matter what they thought on that point, both sides in the 1888 crisis realized that the very meaning and nature of Adventism was at stake in the struggle. Beyond that, both sides came to realize more clearly as time passed that their differences at Minneapolis centered on the meaning of Revelation 14:12.

### 36. What was the standard interpretation of Revelation 14:12 before 1888?

The Adventist interpretation of Revelation 14:12 had been generally consistent before 1888. James White provided a model for that understanding in April 1850. He indicated that the verse had three major points of identification: It indicated (1) a people who were to be patient, despite the disappointment of the 1840s, in waiting for the coming of Jesus; (2) a people who had got "'the victory over the beast, and his image, and over his MARK' and are sealed with the seal of the living God by keeping *'the command- ments of God '";* and (3) a people who "kept the 'faith'" as a body of beliefs in such things as "repentance, faith, baptism, Lord's supper, washing the saints' feet," and so on. A part of keeping the faith, he emphasized, was "KEEPING THE COMMANDMENTS OF GOD." Note that White managed to squeeze commandment keeping into two of the three parts of the verse (PT, April 1850). He was just as explicit in his *Life Incidents* (1868), when he wrote that "there is but one . . . thing to which this term ['the faith of Jesus'] can refer, namely, the precepts and doctrines of our Lord as recorded in the New Testament." That was the faith "which Paul testifies that he had kept (2 Tim. iv, 7)" (p. 259).

J. N. Andrews was of like mind. He stressed the fact that "the faith" or "the faith of Jesus . . . is spoken of as being kept in the same manner that the commandments of God are kept." To him it was important to keep or obey both the commandments of God and the commands of Jesus *(The Three Messages of Revelation XIV,* 5th ed., 135). R. F. Cottrell, another pioneer in Adventist theol- ogy, held the same position. The faith of Jesus, he wrote, "is some- thing that can be obeyed or kept. Therefore we conclude that all that we are required to do in order to be saved from sin belongs to the faith of Jesus" *(Bible Class* 62). "The third message requires faith in all revealed truth, and obedience to all moral law, and to all acts of obedience of faith taught by Christ and his apostles" *(ibid.* 124).

Nearly all Adventist interpretations of Revelation 14:12 before 1888 saw "the faith of Jesus" as a body of truth that one should believe and follow. Most often, however, Adventists gave short shrift to that section of the verse. It was the part about keeping the commandments that got their most devoted attention. Thus, as we noted earlier (question 29), Smith underscored the word *"keep"* when commenting on the text in January 1888, and Butler did the same for *"keep the commandments of God"* in May 1889. Such an emphasis followed from their view that the Sabbath truth, in the context of the mark of the beast, would be God's last message to a world ripe for the Second Coming. It is a slight wonder that such an interpretation and emphasis often led traditional Adventism into the realm of legalism. After all, such implications lay at the foundation of the vocabulary of their faith. Terms such as *keep, do, obey, law,* and *commandments* spelled out in their minds the significance of the Adventist distinctive contribution to Christianity.

It was that interpretation of Revelation 14:12 that came under fire in 1888. *Out of Minneapolis would flow a new significance to the most important Adventist text in the Bible.* That proved to be an earthshaking event for the denomination, and it led to a meaning of Revelation 14:12 that Adventism has yet to understand.

### 37. What new insights on the meaning of the third angel's message emerged from the 1888 General Conference session?

A. T. Jones hinted at the new interpretation in December 1887. "The only way in which they can ever attain to harmony with the righteous law of God," he wrote, "is through the righteousness of God, which is by *faith of Jesus Christ.* . . . In the Third Angel's Message is embodied the supreme truth and the supreme righteousness." He had equated "the supreme truth" with "the commandments of God" and "the supreme righteousness" with "the faith of Jesus" (ST, Dec. 8, 1887).

Ellen White would expand upon Jones's insight in 1888 and beyond. The message given in Minneapolis, she asserted, was "not alone the commandments of God—a part of the third angel's message—but the *faith of Jesus, which comprehends more than is generally supposed.*" The third angel's message needed "to be proclaimed in all its parts. . . . *If we proclaim the commandments of God and leave the other half [the faith of Jesus] scarcely touched, the message is marred in our hands.*"

What Jones and Waggoner presented, she noted, was not anything "new or novel." Rather, "it is an old truth that has been lost sight of." Adventists needed "to bring the faith of Jesus into the right place where it belongs—in the third angel's message. The law has its important position but is powerless unless the righteousness of Christ is placed beside the law to give its glory to the whole royal standard of righteousness. . . . A thorough and complete trust in Jesus will give the right quality to religious experience. Aside from this the experience is nothing. The service is like the offering of Cain—Christless." She went on to talk about Christ's substitutionary death and His blood as the sinner's only hope (EGW MS 30, 1889; italics supplied).

Soon after the Minneapolis meetings Mrs. White made one of her most powerful statements on Revelation 14:12 and the core meaning of Minneapolis. "The third angel's message," she penned, "is the proclamation of the commandments of God *and* the faith of Jesus Christ. *The commandments of God have been proclaimed, but the faith of Jesus Christ has not been proclaimed by Seventh-day Adventists as of equal importance, the law and the gospel going hand in hand.*" She went on to discuss the meaning of the faith of Jesus, which "is talked of, but not understood." *The faith of Jesus, she claimed, means "Jesus becoming our sin-bearer that He might become our sin-pardoning Saviour. . . .* He came to our world and took our sins that we might take His righteousness. *And faith in the ability of Christ to save us amply and fully and entirely is the faith of Jesus."* Adventists, therefore, needed to apply His blood to their lives. By faith they had to lay "hold of the righteousness of Christ."

"Faith in Christ as the sinner's only hope" had been "largely left out, not only of the discourses given but of the religious experience of very many who claim to believe the third angel's message." At Minneapolis, Ellen White recalled, she bore her testimony on "the great subject of the righteousness of Christ connected with the law" as the sinner's "only hope of salvation." That, she emphasized repeatedly, "was not new light to me." She had been preaching it for 44 years, but had not received much positive response from Adventists. Too often, she lamented, their messages were "Christless" (EGW MS 24 1888; italics supplied).

Of particular interest to those seeking to comprehend Ellen White's understanding of Revelation 14:12 and the exact nature of the justification by faith that she approved of in the 1888 message is an article she published in the *Review* during August 1889. In it she wrote that there are "grand truths," including the "doctrine of justification by faith," that many Seventh-day Adventists had lost sight of. At this point in her argument she indicated most vividly what kind of justification by faith had been lost: "The Holiness people have gone to great extremes on this point. With great zeal they have taught, 'Only believe in Christ, and be saved; but away with the law of God.'" She went on to imply that although such people were correct in lifting up salvation by faith, they were wrong in demeaning the law. Because of the imbalance, she wrote, "God has raised up men [Jones and Waggoner] to meet the necessity of this time . . . who will lift up their voice like a trumpet, and show my people their transgressions. . . . *Their work is not only to proclaim the law, but to preach the truth for this time—the Lord our righteousness*" (RH, Aug. 13, 1889; italics supplied).

The preceding passage may be Ellen White's clearest on the meaning and significance of Jones and Waggoner's message. *The genius of their 1888 message was that they had combined the two halves of Revelation 14:12. They not only taught the commandments of God, but they preached the doctrine of faith that the holiness preachers had proclaimed.*

*Thus, from Ellen White's perspective, the importance of the 1888 message was not some special Adventist doctrine of justification by faith developed by Jones and Waggoner. Rather, it was the reuniting of Adventism with basic Christian beliefs on salvation.* She approved of an 1888 message that set forth a Christianity that held up Jesus Christ as the central pillar of all Christian living and thinking, that proclaimed justification through faith (an evangelical belief that Adventists have not been able to improve upon), and that taught sanctification as reflected in obedience to God's law through the power of the Holy Spirit (a point at which nineteenth-century evangelicals often fell short).

Persons holding that the 1888 message of Jones and Waggoner is some unique understanding of salvation not only contradict Waggoner's and Ellen White's plain statements to the contrary (see question 28 above), but they also fail to see what Ellen White actually commended in the presentation of Jones and Waggoner as she relates it to the third angel's message.

For her the faith of Jesus was not a body of beliefs to accept and obey but *faith in* Jesus as Saviour, a concept in line with the Greek of Revelation 14:12, which we can translate as either faith *of* Jesus or faith *in* Jesus.

Such an understanding enables us to comprehend one of Ellen White's most well-known (but often misunderstood) statements on the relationship of righteousness by faith to the third angel's message. "Some of our brethren," she noted in early 1890, "have expressed fears that we shall dwell too much upon the subject of justification by faith." She observed that there would have been no need to emphasize the topic except that Adventists had neglected it in the past, and now that it was being preached, they were "anxious that none of our ministers shall depart from their former manner of teaching the good old doctrines."

Ellen White went on to indicate that "several have written to me, inquiring if the message of justification by faith is the third angel's message, and I have answered, 'It is the third angel's message in verity [i.e., truth]'" (RH, Apr. 1, 1890). Those questioning her were inferring that she had departed from their understanding of the preaching of the third angel. Instead of defending herself, she took the opportunity to state that justification by faith, far from being a diversion from the third angel's message, stood at its very center. *From Ellen White's perspective those who held to the third angel's message would (1) patiently wait for Jesus to return, (2) keep God's commandments while they were waiting, (3) and put their trust and faith in the righteousness of Jesus for their salvation.*

Waggoner hinted at a similar understanding when he indicated that what he had been teaching on the law and gospel was "not a new theory of doctrine" but was "perfectly in harmony with the fundamental principles of truth which have been held not only by our people, but by all the eminent reformers." His gospel teachings were simply "a step nearer the faith of the great Reformers from the days of Paul to the days of Luther and Wesley. It would be a step closer to the heart of the Third Angel's Message" *(Gospel in Galatians* 70).

Thus Waggoner and Mrs. White were in harmony on the fact that the doctrine of justification he set forth, far from being some new understanding of justification, was the belief in justification neglected by Adventists but quite in harmony with the teaching of Paul, Luther, Wesley, and the nineteenth-century holiness preachers.

The contribution of Jones and Waggoner was not some new understanding of justification by faith (see also question 28), but the placing of that teaching within the framework of the third angel's message. As Ellen White so nicely put it, "God has rescued these truths [through Jones and Waggoner] from the companionship of error, and has placed them in their proper framework [i.e., the third angel's message]" (EGW MS 8a, 1888). The two men had brought together the great truths of Adventism centering on the commandments of God and the great truth of evangelical Christianity centering on salvation by faith in Jesus and had placed them in the end-time framework of Revelation 14.

## 38. What are the loud cry and the latter rain, and how has Adventist theology featured them?

The biblical concept of the latter rain is a spiritual analogy based on the Palestinian agricultural year. The early rain fell in the autumn, germinated the seed, and gave crops a start, whereas the latter rain came during the spring and brought the crops to maturity.

In a spiritual sense the early rain began to shower at Pentecost with the outpouring of the Holy Spirit. By analogy the latter rain of the Holy Spirit is to fall just prior to the Second Advent, not only to enable men and women to deepen their Christian experience in preparation for the traumatic end-time events predicted in Revelation but also to empower the church to proclaim its special message to the ends of the earth. Thus both the early and the latter rains have to do with the power of the Holy Spirit.

The loud cry, by way of contrast, is the last message God's people will proclaim to a dying world. The content of that message, according to Ellen White, is the final call to come out of Babylon (Rev. 18:4) united with the third angel's message (GC 604).

Thus the loud cry is God's last message of warning to the world, while the latter rain provides the power needed to proclaim it (see EW 86). Or, as the *Seventh-day Adventist Encyclopedia* puts it, "the latter rain . . . qualifies the church for bearing witness in the 'loud cry'" (1996 ed., vol. 1, 905). Ideally, of course, the two were never to be separated. Unfortunately, as we shall see, the ideal is not always realized.

### 39. In what way did Ellen White relate the loud cry to the 1888 message?

In November 1892 Mrs. White penned that "the time of test is just upon us, for *the loud cry of the third angel has already begun in the revelation of the righteousness of Christ, the sin-pardoning Redeemer.* This is the *beginning* of the light of the angel whose glory shall fill the whole earth. For [i.e., because] it is the work of every one to whom the message of warning has come, *to lift up Jesus,* to present him to the world" (RH, Nov. 22, 1892; italics supplied).

In short, Ellen White held that the loud cry had begun with the proclamation of righteousness by faith in 1888.

**40. Did Ellen White claim that the latter rain had begun in either 1888 or around the time of the 1893 General Conference session?**

Not that we know of from her own records! On the other hand, several preachers, including A. T. Jones, G. B. Starr, and W. W. Prescott, transformed her claim in November 1892 that the loud cry had begun into the idea that the latter rain had begun. Thus Prescott (a foremost colleague of Jones and Waggoner in preaching righteousness by faith in the early 1890s) asserted in early 1893 at the General Conference session that "for four years we have been in the time of the latter rain" (1893 GCB 463). In a similar vein, Jones told the delegates that "'Sister White says that we have been in the time of the latter rain since the Minneapolis meeting'" (ibid. 377).

But what was the source of their information? Not Ellen White but G. B. Starr (ibid.). Thus the double quotation marks used in Jones's statement above. He was quoting Starr rather than Mrs. White. Nowhere do we find her personally claiming that the latter rain had begun in 1888 or 1893. A foundational source for that idea was apparently her statement in November 1892 about the beginning of the loud cry, which her readers quite understandably translated to mean latter rain.

It is important to note, however, that Jones and Prescott had other reasons to believe that the latter rain had begun by the 1893 General Conference session. After all, at that very time they had in their possession testimonies from a second Adventist prophet that they hoped to use to bring about the outpouring of the Holy Spirit before the session was over. Thus Jones could tell the delegates early in the session that God "is not going to be content much longer with one prophet! He will have more. He has done a wonderful work with one. And having done such a great work with one, what in the world will he do when he gets a lot of them?" (ibid. 153).

We will have more to say on the latter rain, the 1893 General Conference session, and Jones's additional prophet in Chapter VII (see especially questions 45, 46, and 47). In the meantime we need to return to the implications of Ellen White's loud cry statement of November 1892.

### 41. What did Ellen White mean when she said that the loud cry had begun in 1888?

We must see the loud cry statement (see question 39) in the light of her repeated assertion that the contribution of Jones and Waggoner was a fuller understanding of Revelation 14:12, especially the "faith of Jesus" as being faith in the uplifted Saviour who died for the sins of the world (see question 37 above).

In essence, Mrs. White was claiming that Seventh-day Adventists at last had a complete understanding of the third angel's message. While they had always grasped the sections of Revelation 14:12 that dealt with waiting patiently for the return of the Lord and the necessity of God's end-time people obeying God's commandments, they had traditionally fallen short on the "faith of Jesus" part of the text. Thus the importance of the contribution of Jones and Waggoner. They had not only preached the Advent and the commandments but also pointed the denomination back to an adequate understanding of righteousness by faith. That is, they had united those aspects of Adventist theology that were distinctively Adventist to the great theme of justification by faith that, as Ellen White put it, was being taught by the holiness preachers (RH, Aug. 13, 1889).

The result was that Adventists since 1888 had finally been in a position to present the third angel's message in all of its fullness and balance. They would no longer leave the other half of the message of Revelation 14:12, in Ellen White's words, "scarcely touched" (EGW MS 30, 1889). Now the faith of Jesus ("Jesus becoming our sin-bearer") and the commandments of God could be "proclaimed by Seventh-day Adventists as of equal importance, the law and the gospel going hand in hand" (EGW MS 24, 1888).

With the understanding of the loud cry as a completed message we can begin to better understand Ellen White's November 1892 statement. If a person reads it at face value, the following ideas are evident: 1). The loud cry began in 1888 with the preaching of the last element of Revelation 14:12—the faith of Jesus. Before that time Adventists had an incomplete message because they did not present the full-orbed gospel that included both the law and the gospel in proper balance. 2). The combining of those two elements by Jones and Waggoner, however, gave the denomination the complete message of Revelation 14:12 that God's people needed to preach before the great harvest of Revelation 14:14-16. Thus 1888 was "the *beginning*" of the loud cry. 3). Why was 1888 the "beginning" of the loud cry? Because ("for") Adventists now had a message of both "warning" (the commandments of God in contrast to the mark of the beast) and of uplifting Jesus. That is what Ellen White said in November 1892. To project into her statement latter-rain concepts (see questions 38 and 40) is to go beyond the facts of the passage.

Waggoner's studies in Romans at the 1891 General Conference session tend to reinforce the conclusions reached in this chapter. After noting that his gospel message was nothing but that given by Paul, he asked if that meant that Adventists needed "to throw away all the doctrines we have preached." "No; by no means," he answered. "Preach them in season and out of season; but, nevertheless, preach nothing but Christ Jesus and him crucified. For if you preach those things without preaching Christ and him crucified, they are shorn of their power." He then went on to devote a great deal of time to how the Adventist distinctive doctrines related to the basic Christian truth of the gospel.

Waggoner concluded with the thought that "the third angel's message is the *whole gospel* of Jesus Christ," including both those "doctrines that make us distinct from the world" and Jesus Christ and Him crucified. The reason that the message had not gone forth in fullness of power, he suggested, was that "in the past many" Adventists "have not had that kernel of the message that it is all Christ. When we have Christ," he claimed, when "we submit ourselves to him, . . . power will rest upon us, and the word that we preach will go with power." "I rejoice tonight," he told the delegates, "in the belief that the loud cry is now beginning" (1891 GCB 238-246).

Mrs. White had been shown the connection of Revelation 14:12 to the loud cry and latter rain in 1886. Writing of the third angel's message as "present truth," she noted that her "guide" had told her that "there is much light yet to shine forth from the law of God [the commandments of God] *and* the gospel of righteousness [the faith of Jesus]. This message [the loud cry], understood in its true character, and proclaimed in the Spirit [the latter rain], will lighten the earth with its glory. . . . The closing work of the third angel's message will be attended with a power that will send the rays of the Sun of Righteousness into all the highways and byways of life" (EGW MS 15, 1888).

From the last two quotations it is evident that Waggoner and Mrs. White quite logically held that latter rain power should accompany the loud cry message. Did it? If not, why not? It is to those questions that we now turn.

## 42. If the Adventists in 1892 and 1893 had the loud cry, where was the latter rain?

Our question has primarily two answers. The first A. T. Jones and others set forth at the 1893 General Conference session. They held that God was already pouring out the latter rain and all that the church had to do was to accept the power being offered at the 1893 meetings (see questions 46 and 47). Some twentieth-century Adventists, including the leaders of the 1888 Message Study Committee, have accepted that answer. As a result they feel that the denomination made a major error in rejecting Jones's invitation to the latter rain in 1893. We will examine the validity of this position in our next chapter.

Ellen White presented the second answer. She never accused the denomination specifically of rejecting Jones's version of the latter rain in 1893, but she did indicate that even though the denomination had received the loud cry message in 1888, the ugly spirit exhibited in the battle over the law in Galatians and other issues had blocked the outpouring of the latter rain power. "By exciting that opposition," she wrote to Smith in 1896, "Satan succeeded in shutting away from our people, in a great measure, the special power of the Holy Spirit that God longed to impart to them. The enemy prevented them from obtaining that efficiency [the latter rain] which might have been theirs in carrying the truth [the loud cry message] to the world, as the apostles proclaimed it after the day of Pentecost. The light that is to lighten the whole earth with its glory [the loud cry message energized by the latter rain power] was resisted, and by the action of our own brethren has been in a great degree kept away from the world" (EGW to US, June 6, 1896).

Thus we can conclude that even though the loud cry began in 1888, the power to preach it in fullness has been delayed for the past 100 years.

Why? Ellen White suggests that a central problem is the need to overcome the "spirit of Minneapolis" (see question 15) by fully internalizing the love of Christ. In 1888 she noted that "it has been Satan's studied work to keep the love of Christ out of our hearts. . . . *What we want is the love of Christ, to love God supremely and our neighbor as ourselves. When we have this, there will be a breaking down as with the walls of Jericho before the children of Israel"* (1888 Materials 159). Again she penned: "When those who profess the name of Christ shall practice the principles of the golden rule, the same power will attend the gospel as in apostolic times" (MB 137).

In conclusion, the greatest need of Adventism today is the same as it was in the 1880s. In 1887 Mrs. White commented that "a revival of true godliness among us is the greatest and most urgent of all our needs. . . . There must be earnest effort to obtain the blessing of the Lord, not because God is not willing to bestow His blessing upon us, but because we are unprepared to receive it" (RH, Mar. 22, 1887). The great need of Adventism since 1888 is the same as it was before that memorable General Conference session. It is not more doctrinal precision, but the daily living of God's love in a practical way. Truth is good, but it needs to be validated by a joyful and caring Christianity that avoids the spirit of Minneapolis by exuding the spirit of Jesus. It is that type of Christianity that Ellen White ties to latter rain power.

# CHAPTER 7

# MOVING AWAY FROM MINNEAPOLIS: PERSONALITIES AND EVENTS

Just as the General Conference session prepared to close, a disgruntled G. I. Butler sent in his resignation as president of the denomination. Smith also soon gave up his position as General Conference secretary. The denomination elected O. A. Olsen, then in Europe, to the presidency. S. N. Haskell was to serve as interim president until Olsen could wind up his affairs and come to the United States. Haskell, however, managed to evade the job, and it went to W. C. White while he was out of the room conferring with his mother. "This was quite a shock to me," the retiring Willie related, "and almost made me sick." To his wife he wrote that it was not only "much against" his will, but it "was about the bitterest pill that I have had to take, and it seems as though some of us have been taking pills ever since we set foot on Minneapolis soil" (WCW to JNL, Nov. 20, 1888; WCW to MW, Nov. 19, 24, 1888).

While the non-Adventist St. Paul *Pioneer Press* on November 2 noted that the session was "unusually animated" and characterized by "the utmost harmony," Ellen White perceived it as the "most incomprehensible tug of war we have ever had among our people" and as "one of the saddest chapters in the history of the believers in present truth." Despite that opinion, she believed that "this meeting will result in great good. . . . The truth will triumph and we mean to triumph with it" (EGW to MW, Nov. 4, 1888; EGW to CPB, Nov. 19, 1902).

W. C. White noted shortly after the conference that the delegates returned home with "a great variety of sentiments. Some felt that it had been the greatest blessing of their lives; others, that it marked the beginning of a period of darkness, and that the evil effects of what had been done at the conference could never be effaced." He personally believed God would work out things for the good of the church (WCW to JNL, Nov. 20, 1888).

### 43. Given the fact that Jones, Waggoner, and Ellen White had such a poor reception among the leaders at the 1888 General Conference session, what steps did they take to spread their "most precious message"?

Ellen White left Minneapolis discouraged with the ministerial leadership of the denomination, but she still had hope in the Adventist people as a whole. Before the close of the conference she had told the assembled ministers that if they would not accept the light, she wanted to "give the people a chance; perhaps they may receive it" (EGW MS 9, 1888). They certainly needed it. In September 1889 she would remark that "there is not one in one hundred" who really understood what it meant to be justified by faith, what it meant that "Christ should be . . . the only hope and salvation" (RH, Sept. 3, 1889). Up through the fall of 1891 she, Jones, and Waggoner would tour the nation, preaching righteousness by faith to "the people" and to the ministry. After she left for Australia in 1891 and Waggoner had gone to England, Jones and W. W. Prescott continued to present the message in the United States. All through this period and beyond it, Ellen White emphasized that God had chosen Jones and Waggoner to bear a special message to the Adventist Church, and she published widely on the topic of righteousness by faith herself.

The new General Conference administrations of O. A. Olsen (1888-1897) and George A. Irwin (1897-1901) responded positively to Mrs. White's endorsement by giving Jones and Waggoner broad exposure throughout the 1890s. They had access to the people through the churches, the Sabbath school lessons, the colleges, the in-service schools regularly held for the ministry, and the denomination's publishing houses. Especially important was the fact that during each General Conference session from 1889 through 1897 Jones and Waggoner received the leading role in the study of the Bible and theology (see the section on Jones and Waggoner under question 49). Beyond that, the fact that the denomination made Jones editor of the *Review* (with Smith as his assistant) in 1897 (that would have taken place in 1894, but Jones's problem with Anna Rice delayed it) was more than symbolic. As the denomination's foremost editor, Jones used the *Review* as a channel for his teachings.

As early as February 1890, R. A. Underwood (an opponent of Jones and Waggoner) would complain to Olsen that Waggoner had had the "widest possible berth both in public and in print that the denomination could give him to present his views . . . untrammeled" (RAU to OAO, Feb. 7, 1890). Such a statement would have been even more true (especially for Jones) during the middle and late nineties. It would have been hard to conceive of a program that could have given the reformers more prominence during the 1890s.

## 44. What was the response to the widespread preaching of Jones, Waggoner, and Ellen White?

The months following Minneapolis were strenuous for Mrs. White and her colleagues as they preached Christ and His love to Adventist ministry and laity across the nation. While the results were far from those desired, some confessions regarding a wrong attitude at Minneapolis did occur as well as a fair amount of rejoicing over newly found freedom in Christ's righteousness. Mrs.

White joyfully wrote during the 1889 General Conference session that they were "having most excellent meetings. The spirit that was in the meeting at Minneapolis is not here." Many of the delegates testified that the past year had "been the best of their life; the light shining forth from the Word of God has been clear and distinct—justification by faith, Christ our righteousness" (3SM 160).

While the 1889 session was a milestone in that it represented a marked improvement over 1888, the battle in many ways was just beginning. A major breakthrough would take place in March 1890 at the ministers' school. The denomination regularly held such institutes for several years after 1888 because the ministerial response at Minneapolis had highlighted an inability to relate to the Bible and the great truths of Christianity. The faculty included leading proponents from both sides of the 1888 conflict. The 1890 ministers' school struggled through the winter in an atmosphere of controversy, doubt, and renewed suspicion over the purported California conspiracy. The major bone of theological contention had been the covenants, a topic that Waggoner's Sabbath school lessons had recently reignited. A series of explanations by Ellen White and Jones and Waggoner that cleared up the rumor of the California conspiracy (see question 9) led to many confessions concerning the harboring of a wrong spirit since the 1888 meetings.

The breakthrough overjoyed denominational president O. A. Olsen, a supporter of Jones and Waggoner. "I think," he claimed on March 20, "I can say now that the prospects for a better understanding and greater unity were never so good for several years. Many that have felt greatly perplexed, are feeling much relieved, and light is coming in, where darkness has previously existed" (OAO to GCT, Mar. 20, 1890). From that time on much of the heat of the controversy subsided and many began to place renewed trust in Ellen White. Many had begun "to understand," wrote O. A. Olsen, "that the testimony has not been so much to blame as they had thought, but that the fault was with ourselves and our giving credence to reports, rather than to the truth and the spirit of God" (OAO to LTN, Mar. 11, 1890).

We should note, however, that even though significant victories did take place in the early 1890s as Adventists accepted righteousness by faith and overcame the spirit of Minneapolis, not all the problems of faith or attitude cleared up. Significant tension remained in the church throughout the nineties and into the twentieth century (for more on the acceptance and/or rejection of the 1888 message, see question 50).

### 45. What effect did the continuing Sunday law crisis have on the church?

In question 4 we noted the growing tension over Sunday laws throughout the 1880s that culminated in the spring of 1888 with the attempts of Senator H. W. Blair to get a constitutional amendment to Christianize America's public schools and to pass national Sunday legislation. Blair's Sunday sacredness bill was the first attempt at Sunday legislation in the United States since the 1830s. The Sunday bill failed in 1888, but Blair put it before the Senate again in 1889. As with the 1888 bill, it went down after a hard fight in which Adventists played a prominent role. In 1890 W.C.P. Breckenridge sponsored Sunday legislation in the House of Representatives. It also did not pass.

In the meantime, between the early 1880s and 1895 scores of Adventists faced arrest in the United States (as well as overseas) for violating state Sunday laws. The most publicized case was that of R. M. King, who had his case appealed to the United States Supreme Court. King, however, avoided making constitutional history by dying in November 1891 while his case was still on the Court's docket.

The local authorities treated many of the arrested Adventists as common criminals. Their trials received major coverage in the nation's foremost newspapers. J. N. Loughborough, speaking of the publicity generated by the King case, wrote that "within one month, the central truth of the third angel's message was brought to the attention of more people than we had been able to reach in more than twenty years" *(Rise and Progress of SDAs* 362). It is no wonder that the denomination began to talk about the imminence of the latter rain and the loud cry.

By 1892 King was dead and the Blair and Breckenridge bills had failed, but the Sunday forces could not be held at bay indefinitely. August 5, 1892, saw President Benjamin Harrison sign the United States' first national Sunday law. It stipulated that the Chicago World's Fair would not receive any federal appropriations unless the fair closed on Sunday.

The sequence of events leading up to the August 1892 Sunday law looked ominous to Seventh-day Adventists. On February 18 Ellen White wrote in Australia that *"Protestantism is now reaching hands across the gulf to clasp hands with [the] papacy, and a confederacy is being formed to trample out of sight the Sabbath of the fourth commandment.* . . . Something great and decisive is to take place, and that right early"* (EGW MS 27, 1892; italics supplied).

Eleven days later the United States Supreme Court gave its ruling in *Church of the Holy Trinity v. United States. Holy Trinity* was fraught with great meaning for the Adventist interpretation of prophecy, since the Court unanimously asserted in its ruling that *the United States "is a Christian nation."* As a part of its argument the Court supplied evidence from the nation's "laws, its business, its customs and its society." *That evidence included "the laws respecting the observance of the Sabbath [Sunday]"* (A. P. Stokes, *Church and State in the U.S.,* vol. 3, 570, 572; italics supplied).

Not surprisingly, the Sunday forces regarded that declaration as a green light for the constitutionality of a national Sunday law. The National Reform Association rejoiced in the ruling. " 'Christianity is the law of the land,' " it proclaimed while quoting the Court. "The Christian church, therefore, has rights in this country. Among these is the right to one day in seven . . . that it may be devoted to worship of . . . God" *(Christian Statesman,* May 21, 1892, quoted in ATJ, *Appeal From the U.S. Supreme Court Decision,* 40). Thus *Holy Trinity* became a major piece of artillery in the siege of the Sunday forces on Congress during the spring and summer of 1892.

The Battle Creek Adventists did not know of either Ellen White's February 18 statement or of *Holy Trinity* for several months. But by the middle of May A. T. Jones came into possession of both pieces of information. Combined with the Adventist interpretation of prophecy, they made an explosive package. On May 14 and 21, 1892, he preached two sermons in Battle Creek that electrified his audience by claiming that the image of the beast had been formed on February 29 in the Court's *Holy Trinity* ruling. "All that remains," he asserted, "is to give life to it by the enforcement of whatever religious observances any bigots may choose, who can control the civil power" (RH, May 31, 1892). He pointed out that Adventists had preached this event for 40 years. Now it was time to get ready. After all, he proclaimed, "it is nothing but the unbelief of our own people that keeps back the loud cry of the third angel's message to-day" (RH, June 21, 1892). Any Adventist who did not agree with him, he claimed, was not "qualified" to sound the "message of warning" against the worship of the beast (RH, June 14, 1892). That statement was undoubtedly a backhanded reference to Uriah Smith, who Jones believed was too cautious in his prophetic interpretations.

The *Review* published Jones's sermons, but Smith could not restrain himself from taking a public swat at him. In the issue that contained the last of Jones's sermons, the *Review* editor included an article that denied that the image had been formed, or that *Holy Trinity* had changed anything.

The public controversy over the image had the effect of polarizing the Adventist leadership. It was Minneapolis all over again to General Conference president Olsen. Since 1888, he complained, "there has been a sort of watching one another's expressions, and taking advantage of certain utterances" (OAO to SNH, July 25, 1892). Both sides were apparently guilty of that problem. The spirit of Minneapolis refused to die.

Meanwhile, on August 5 President Benjamin Harrison signed the World's Fair national Sunday law. The quill used in the signing, placed in a silk-lined case, went to the president of the

American Sabbath Union. It was a high day for the Sunday forces. *The signing, Jones claimed, gave life to the image* (RH, Aug. 9, 1892; SNH to OAO, Sept. 12, 1892). That interpretation merely widened the distance between him and Smith. The denomination's periodicals settled down to a cold war in which the *Signs of the Times*, the *American Sentinel*, and the *Home Missionary* supported Jones's interpretation of the image, while the *Review* largely ignored both Jones and the topic.

Ellen White made no effort to decide the issue, even though she counseled Jones to "avoid all impression[s] which savor of extremes" and she rebuked Smith for not caring enough to talk over the differences of interpretation privately with the younger man (EGW to ATJ, Sept. 2, 1892; EGW to US, Aug. 30, 1892).

While refusing to settle the interpretive battle between Jones and Smith, Mrs. White had no doubt that the denomination was facing the end of time. Speaking of the Sunday crisis in the late 1880s, she penned that *"the most momentous struggle of all the ages is just before us. Events which for more than forty years we have upon the authority of the prophetic word declared to be impending are now taking place"* (5T 711; italics supplied). In the December 6, 1892, *Review* she claimed that the world and the church were "on the very eve of the crisis." Such statements from her and most other denominational leaders filled the Adventist air as the 1893 General Conference session convened in Battle Creek a few weeks later.

Thus pillar number one was in place for end-time excitement at the 1893 General Conference session to open in February. Ellen White's November 22, 1892, *Review* article, which claimed that the loud cry had begun with the preaching of Christ's righteousness in 1888 (see questions 39-42) did not lessen the excitement. Confusing the loud cry (a message) with the latter rain (an outpouring of the power of the Holy Spirit—a person), Jones preached "a stirring sermon on the 'latter rain' and the loud cry of the third angel's message" in late November in the Battle Creek Tabernacle (WAS to EJW, Nov. 28, 1892; see questions 38-41). Revival immediately broke out in the Adventist ranks. With that sermon a major piece had fallen into place for the 1893 General Conference session. Ellen White's November 22 loud cry statement (question 39) would be the dominating "text" of those meetings.

But the Sunday crisis and Ellen White's loud cry statement were not the only reasons the 1893 revivalists (Jones and Prescott) were excited about the latter rain. They had also received a testimony from a woman whom they had *already* come to accept as a prophet.

### 46. What part did the Anna Rice excitement play in the latter rain expectations of 1893?

Anna Rice (sometimes called Anna Phillips) played a significant role in the 1893 expectations even though few have understood her part. Her influence, however, was not direct. Rather it came through the agencies of A. T. Jones and W. W. Prescott.

Sometime in 1892 Rice began to have visionary experiences. It was only natural for her to wonder if they were genuine. As a result, in the latter half of 1892 she traveled from the West Coast to Chicago to meet with Jones to determine whether she was a true prophet. Her method, S. N. Haskell wrote to Ellen White, was quite straightforward: "You saw some time ago that Bro. Jones and Waggoner had advanced light for this people; and therefore, if A. T. Jones should endorse them [Anna's visions] it would settle it in her mind that they were of God." Upon Jones's positive reception of her, Anna was settled that her calling was "of the Lord" (SNH to EGW, Jan. 4, 189[3]). That approval became central to both Anna's future ministry and Jones's course of action in 1893 and 1894 (see question 23).

Because of his acceptance of Anna's work, Jones could tell his hearers on September 29, 1893, at the Michigan camp meeting that "there are going to be more prophets before the third angel's message closes." He went on to note that a person could test such prophets by recognizing God's voice in them. That was a safe test, Jones asserted, because *"the devil cannot imitate the voice of Jesus Christ.* No, sir . . . He may speak in the very *words* that are in the Bible, but it is not the *voice* of Jesus. No sir." Jones, therefore, exhorted his hearers to learn to recognize the voice of God, since His sheep will know His voice and follow Him (HM Extra, November 1893).

Soon after Jones's acceptance of Anna's work in 1892, Ellen White came out with her statement that the loud cry had already begun (question 39). It was only natural that Jones should see Anna Rice's visions in the light of that statement and conclude that the latter rain had begun (question 40).

During the 1893 General Conference meetings in February 1893 Anna sent at least two letters to Jones. The first was on February 7. It accompanied a testimony to her adopted parents, dated August 10, 1892. Her second letter to Jones carried the date of February 21, 1893. It was actually a "testimony" calling for repentance and reform in Adventist lifestyle—a summons to more perfect Christian living in the light of the imminence of the Second Coming. Jones desired to read the Rice "testimonies" to the delegates of the 1893 General Conference session, but the General Conference president forbade him to do so (CMR to LTN, Mar. 22, 1894).

*It must have grated upon Jones's sensitive nature to be restricted in bringing about the latter rain through the reading of Anna's testimonies. All he could do was hint at that exciting "fulfillment of prophecy" that was propelling him and Prescott in their conviction that the latter rain had already begun. "Thank the Lord," Jones told the delegates at the General Conference session, "he is not going to be content much longer with one prophet! He will have more.* He has done a wonderful work with one. And having done such a great work with one, what in the world will he do when he gets a lot of them." He then quoted Joel 2 (1893 GCB 153; italics supplied).

But even though Jones was forbidden to read Anna's testimonies at the 1893 General Conference session, he did not put them aside. In mid-1893, for example, Jones and Prescott were quite sure they were hearing the voice of God in Anna's testimonies. They would publicly read a selection from Ellen White and then one from Anna Rice, asking their congregation after each whether they heard the voice. The answer was invariably positive. The president of the Kansas Conference reported that Jones had read a Rice testimony at his camp meeting in September 1893, and not one in 100 could tell that it was not from Ellen White (LTN to OAO, Mar. 2, 1894; CMR to LTN, [1894]).

What Jones could not do in the General Conference president's presence at the 1893 session, he would do in his absence. In December 1893, with Olsen 12,000 miles away in Australia, Jones and Prescott would use the Anna Rice testimony penned to Jones on February 21 to start a "real" outpouring of the Spirit in the Battle Creek church. The excitement stimulated by the reading of that "testimony" began what may have been the greatest "revival" in the history of the Battle Creek Adventist community. The results immediately following his presentation of the Rice material in the Battle Creek Tabernacle were an offering equivalent to $600,000 to $800,000 in today's purchasing power, a large number of baptisms, and a sprouting up of what Leroy T. Nicola (secretary of the General Conference) called prophecy "cranks" and others with supposed charismatic gifts—including one person with the "gift of 'roaring.'" The Anna Rice movement threatened to take Adventism by storm during the first two months of 1894, but by March Ellen White had exposed it as a misplaced enthusiasm and Jones and Prescott were repenting of their leadership in it (see GRK, *From 1888 to Apostasy*, 104-116, for a discussion of the Rice movement).

Adventists can be thankful that Jones did not receive a free hand at the 1893 session, since by that time he was not a totally reliable guide. His "latter rain revival" might have led Adventism down strange paths indeed, and it could have changed the nature of the Seventh-day Adventist Church by moving it closer to the then-developing Pentecostalism. (Along that line, it is of more than passing interest that Jones's last religious affiliation would be with a group of tongues-speaking, Sabbathkeeping Pentecostals. He never did escape his desire for the charismatic.)

S. N. Haskell noted that many accepted Jones and Prescott's interpretation of the loud cry and the latter rain in 1893. That acceptance paved the way, he pointed out, for the rapid and widespread acceptance of Anna Rice's prophetic role in early 1894.

Haskell also indicated that such people saw Anna's visions as "the increasing of the gift of prophecy," and thus "a sign of the outpouring of the Spirit of God" (SNH to EGW, May 26, 1894).

*The actual course of events, as documented above, directly contradicts the interpretation of some who point back to 1893 as a time when the denominational leaders rejected the genuine latter rain.* For example, Robert J. Wieland and Donald K. Short have the sequence of events backward when they write that "there were prophesyings of a sort after this session [1893], and both Prescott and Jones were deceived by the unfortunate claims of one Anna Rice Phillips. Fanaticism was inevitable, *for the loud cry of the third angel's message did not go forth after the 1893 session.*" As a result, these influential authors suggest, "the session clearly marked the withdrawal of Heaven's gift of the latter rain" *(1888 Re-examined,* rev. ed., 110, 91).

Contrary to that interpretation, *the facts indicate that Jones and Prescott had been "deceived" before the beginning of the 1893 meetings* and that it was the denominational leadership that blocked any moves of the reformers that might have led to fanatical excitement during the session itself. *We must emphasize again that neither Jones nor Prescott were entirely reliable guides in matters of the Holy Spirit by the time of the 1893 meetings.* While we do not know all the reasons for the delay of the Second Advent, it was apparently not a rejection of A. T. Jones's version of the latter rain in 1893. Even though he and Prescott had many Christ-centered insights during the early 1890s, not all they taught was "pure gold."

## 47. What kind of atmosphere pervaded the 1893 General Conference meetings?

It was charged with an immediate anticipation of the Second Coming. Jones and Prescott were especially ebullient throughout the meetings. With the Sunday law crisis, Ellen White's loud cry statement, and the revelation of a new prophet in hand they were certain they were in the final days of earth's history.

But Jones and Prescott were not alone. Much of the denomination's leadership shared the same mind-set. Present-day Adventism would be beside itself with anticipatory excitement if it had even 10 percent of the indicators of prophetic fulfillment that faced the delegates to the 1893 session.

Ellen White was certainly impressed with the prophetic signs. On January 9, 1893, she penned a letter to William Ings that expressed her thoughts. *"The time of peril is now upon us. It can no longer be spoken of as in the future."* She went on to rebuke those who had opposed Jones and Waggoner since 1888, noting that their resistance had "tended to make of no effect the light God had given to his people through the Testimonies." Furthermore, she deplored the division within the Adventist ranks in which "men of the same faith, in the same city, turn their weapons against each other." Such a condition of things was an "astonishment to the heavenly universe." *"If every soldier of Christ had done his duty, if every watchman on the walls of Zion had given the trumpet a certain sound, the world might ere this have heard the message of warning.* But the work is years behind."

Part of that letter was read to the conference delegates on February 27. The unread portion, while suggesting that Jones may have been premature in his statement concerning the formation of the image, definitely faulted Smith's course of action and commended Jones for having a timely message for the "starving flock of God." Ellen White claimed that "the Lord is soon to come." The letter also expressed no softening of her comments regarding the retarding influence of those who had resisted the 1888 experience (EGW to WI, Jan. 9, 1893; italics supplied).

The imminence of the Second Advent and the rejection of the 1888 experience were the focal points of Jones and Prescott at the 1893 meetings. Prescott had 10 sermons on the promise of the Holy Spirit, while Jones had 24 discourses on the third angel's message. Their presentations dovetailed as both men emphasized that the denomination had been in the time of the loud cry since 1888, and that God was ready to pour out His Spirit upon a repentant church (see questions 39, 40, and 41).

Prescott had no doubt that a "work that will be greater than

Pentecost has begun." The 1893 General Conference session, he proclaimed, would fit the leaders of the church for the closing work. The church had failed at Minneapolis. Using Christ's illustration of the unfruitful tree, he pointed out that Jesus did not cut it down at the end of three years. In mercy He gave it a fourth year. It had been four years since Minneapolis, Prescott told his attentive audience. Now was the deciding moment—the time of shaking for the Adventist Church. The present-day church needed to pray just as intently for the Holy Spirit as did the apostolic church at Pentecost. "It seems to me," he told the delegates, "that right now we are making choices that will determine whether we [as individuals] shall go on with this work through the loud cry and be translated, or whether we shall be deceived by the devices of Satan and be left out in darkness, and the work go on without us." Prescott was not certain that another General Conference session would ever convene. Time was short indeed (1893 GCB 39, 65, 105, 384, 386, 504).

O. A. Olsen backed up Prescott and Jones, telling the delegates that the church was not prepared for the loud cry because its ministers had still not imbibed the message of 1888 as anything but a theory. They could preach the doctrines, but they could not lead sinners to Christ because they did not have a "living connection" with Him themselves (*ibid.* 188, 189).

In his sermons, Jones captured and illustrated the unity of righteousness by faith and religious liberty inherent in the three angels' messages of Revelation 14. After preaching several sermons on the forming of the image to the beast and its significance, he pointed out that the next thing Adventists should look for was the wrath of God. After all, they were already in the time of the loud cry. Thus, they soon could expect the seven last plagues and the Second Coming. *"The time is exceedingly short."* The church, therefore, must totally separate itself from the world. Health reform would prepare the members for translation. The death penalty hovered over them, and they should force the hand of the persecutors by continuing to work on Sunday. Not to do so was to worship the beast through his commandment to observe the first day of the week *(ibid.* 87, 88, 115, 123, 89, 125, 126).

Jones was certain that the church had not yet received the latter rain—to any great extent at least. That was because so many had resisted the Minneapolis experience and did not possess Christ as both their justification and sanctification. Accepting the centrality of Christ as preached at Minneapolis, he suggested, was crucial because only the pure can receive the latter rain. When Minneapolis rejected experiential faith in Christ, it in essence spurned the loud cry and the latter rain *(ibid.* 377, 183, 184, 243, 494, 167, 179).

"This meeting," Jones asserted, must be the time of decision for each delegate. When they received righteousness by faith they would also acquire the latter rain. His appeals brought confessions from many who still harbored bitterness from Minneapolis. No one, Jones claimed, needed to leave the General Conference session without receiving the Holy Spirit *(ibid.* 377, 499).

"Get ready to meet Him [Jesus]," he urged in his final sermon, "for He is coming. Get ready to be like Him; for that glory of which He has given us a part now will make us like Him altogether in that day" *(ibid.* 523).

Like Prescott, Jones was convinced that the conference would not close without a mighty outpouring of the Spirit. He could not "risk" being absent from any of the meetings, he told the delegates, because he could not tell "at what meeting the Spirit may be poured upon us" *(ibid.* 400). Jones had preached mightily and convincingly, and many had made confessions regarding their resistance at Minneapolis, but still the outpouring had not come.

The 1893 General Conference session was undoubtedly an impressive event. The issue of what went right or wrong at those meetings may never be solved historically to everyone's satisfaction, but of two things we can be certain. First, it was a time of unprecedented and unrepeated end-time anticipation. The signs of the times of prophetic fulfillment were on every hand, but without the full realization of those expectations. A second solid conclusion is that one can hardly agree with Robert Wieland when all the facts are taken into consideration. In 1988 he wrote that "what was rejected by the leadership [of the church] was not the doctrine of righteousness by faith, but the beginning of the latter rain" *(Ministry,* June 1988). That statement, as noted in question 46, could be true only if one is willing to accept the testimonies of Anna Rice as a part of that latter rain. Thus, even though church leadership undoubtedly made failures in 1893, those failures are hardly the ones asserted by certain individuals and groups with an interest in the 1888 message.

## 48. What contribution did the 1895 General Conference meetings make to the evolving theology of Jones and Waggoner?

Another General Conference session that has loomed large in the controversy over 1888 is that of 1895. Jones preached some 26 times on the third angel's message at that conference. The meetings have assumed importance in Adventist discussions largely because his sermons contain what may be the most complete discussion by either Jones or Waggoner on the nature of Christ in relation to righteousness by faith. Jones did his best to demonstrate that Christ's nature was "precisely" that of the fallen Adam. In the face of an Ellen White statement claiming that Christ "is a brother in our infirmities, but not in possessing like passions" (2T 202), however, he found himself forced to admit that Christ was like Adam physically, but not spiritually, since He did not possess fallen humanity's mind or passions (1895 GCB 231-233, 436, 312, 327-333). Despite the fact that Jones had to admit that Jesus had "precisely our nature" only in terms of His flesh, he continued to teach his original position, apparently not realizing that he had given up the essential point of his argument. We will return to our discussion of Christ's human nature and its relation to the teachings of Jones and Waggoner in questions 52 and 53.

## 49. What became of the four major Minneapolis contestants?
*G. I. Butler*

Butler, feeling that he had been "slaughtered" in the house of his friends (GIB to EGW, Oct. 1, 1888), gave up the General

Conference presidency at the conclusion of the Minneapolis session. Soon after the 1888 meetings he and his wife went into untimely retirement from all denominational work. He styled his leaving the leadership of the church as "Health-Seeking in Florida" (RH, Jan. 15, 1889). Six days before his departure for the South in mid-December, Ellen White sent him a letter in which she called him an enemy of the Testimonies and an unconverted man. She closed it with an appeal to his heart to change his ways (EGW to GIB and wife, Dec. 11, 1888).

Mrs. White sent many more letters that repeatedly pleaded with Butler to confess his waywardness in the events leading up to Minneapolis. Butler, however, was not up to confessions, at least for a few years. Looking back at his early Florida period from the perspective of 1905, he wrote: "Some people find it very hard to make a confession. I cannot and will not make a confession, as I have told Sister White, over and over again, when I was in Florida, that I could not see to be right, and justly required of me. She used to write me, over and over, about the Minneapolis meeting, and things of that kind, and I invariably wrote right back to her that it was utterly useless for me to go to making confessions I did not believe were called for. I stood my ground on that, through and through. I was put in a close and trying place, believing as I do, in her Testimonies." He would, he claimed, never make the mistake of claiming peace when it did not exist (GIB to JHK, June 11, 1905).

To outward appearances, Butler's frustration had reached its peak in early 1893 when he asked that the denomination not renew his ministerial credentials. (That was undoubtedly the only such request by an ex-president in the history of the General Conference.) The General Conference in session refused to grant the petition (OAO to GIB, Mar. 31, 1893).

In actuality Butler was probably not requesting to resign as a minister as much as he was sending out a question that he needed to have answered—"Am I still needed?" The reason came out several months later. The Christian denomination in his neighborhood had invited him to their new church dedication. Soon after, by unanimous vote, they offered him the privilege of holding services in the building when the congregation was not using it. Butler "took this as an indication that the Lord wanted him to move out and do some preaching." As a result, he spoke to a congregation for the first time in four years. That was the beginning, he claimed, of "the old fire and love . . . springing up in his heart." It was at that juncture, apparently, that Butler had sent up his trial balloon regarding his credentials. Before long he asked for a tent and an assistant so that he could continue to hold meetings in case he lost the use of the Christian church building (OAO to EGW, July 23, 1893; OAO to LHC, June 21, 1893; OAO to GIB, June 26, 1893).

Overjoyed with his acceptance, Butler declared that he was almost ready to exclaim that "the dear brethren have entered into a conspiracy to kill the old sinner with kindness." He still could not believe, however, "that God led Waggoner to deluge the denomination with the Galatians controversy," but he claimed that God had brought good out of it—especially in terms of the increased prominence of justification by faith and the righteousness of Christ. In June 1893 Butler published his new position in the *Review,* noting that God had blessed the denomination in the agitation over "the necessity of appropriating Christ's righteousness by faith." He reported that he "freely indorsed [sic]" what he had previously resisted (GIB to SNH, Apr. 22, 1893; RH, June 13, 1893).

In a private letter the ex-president acknowledged that it had probably been best for him to leave the work of the church for a time, since he had finally become convinced by Ellen White that he had hindered its progress. "The past few years," he judged, had "pretty effectually broken my back, but that is a small matter compared with the progress of the work" (GIB to SNH, Apr. 22, 1893). By the autumn of 1894 Butler was even inviting A. T. Jones to help him at the Florida camp meeting.

In 1901, after his wife's death, Butler came out of semiretirement to become president of the Florida Conference. Between 1902 and 1907 he served as president of the Southern Union Conference.

Ellen White rejoiced to see the aged pioneer back in a position of leadership. "I have known," she told the delegates at the 1903 General Conference session, "that the time would come when he would again take his place in the work. I want you to appreciate the trials that he has passed through. . . . God desires the gray-haired pioneers" who had a part in early Adventism "to stand in their place in His work today. They are not to drop out of sight." The new Butler, she wrote in 1902, was not the same man he had been in 1888. Not only was he "strong in physical and spiritual health," but "the Lord has proved and tested and tried him, as he did Job and as he did Moses. I see in Elder Butler one who has humbled his soul before God. He has another spirit than the Elder Butler of younger years. He has been learning his lesson at the feet of Jesus" (1903 GCB 205; EGW to Brother and Sister Keck, May 1902).

Such a bill of health did not mean that Butler was straight on the main issues of 1888. In 1910, after Jones and Waggoner had departed from the denomination, A. G. Daniells reported a conversation he had had with Butler in late 1909. "He spoke especially of their [Jones and Waggoner's] position on the laws and covenants, and then pointed to the course they are now taking, and told me, with considerable emphasis, that he never could see light in their special messages, and that he had never taken [t]his position." Butler had still not come to terms, Daniells added, with Ellen White's position on the covenants in *Patriarchs and Prophets*. Whereas she claimed that Christ's righteousness saved the Old Testament saints, "obey and live" was still a part of Butler's theology (AGD to WCW, Jan. 21, 1910).

Despite his problems, Ellen White could write to the old warrior in 1910 that she had not lost faith in him. He may not have been able to transcend his pre-1888 beliefs and fears, and he may not have seen things the same as she, but she accepted the sincerity of his heart. Thus it had been when he differed with her over the Kellogg crisis in 1905—a threatening problem of the highest magnitude. "Though he may make some mistakes," she remarked at that time, "yet he is a servant of the living God, and I shall do all I possibly can to sustain him in his work." Ellen White was apparently more interested in him as a person and in his improved attitude than she was in the impeccableness of his theology (see question 34). He had, she claimed in 1910, an important witness for the denomination's younger ministers (EGW to GIB, Nov. 23, 1910; EGW to JEW, Sept. 26, 1905). Remaining surprisingly active in the church, Butler died in 1918.

*Uriah Smith*

Like Butler, Smith underwent a traumatic experience at the Minneapolis meetings. Deeply disappointed and upset by the session, he resigned from his long-held position as General Conference secretary in November 1888. Not being quite as bold as Butler, however, he held on to the editorship of the *Review*. He would maintain that post until 1897, sparring with Jones for much of the time over prophetic interpretation and other issues. His editorship during those years, however, was a downhill battle in the face of the popularity of the charismatic Jones, who had become the most listened to ministerial voice in Adventism by late 1892. In 1897 Smith received his ultimate humiliation when the denomination appointed him as Jones's assistant editor on the *Review* staff.

Smith found it next to impossible to come to grips with the fact that Waggoner had preached the ten-commandment view of Galatians at Minneapolis and that Ellen White had backed Waggoner on the relation of law and gospel. Waggoner's publication of the Galatians articles in the mid-1880s in the *Signs,* Smith often repeated, was one of the worst things that had ever happened to the denomination. Largely because of the Galatians issue, Smith rejected everything Waggoner stood for.

Smith was not only upset with Waggoner, but also at odds with Ellen White in the post-1888 period for supporting the younger men at Minneapolis. For the next few years after Minneapolis, Smith would be a ringleader in casting doubt upon Ellen White's work. As with Butler, Mrs. White often appealed to Smith, but he was intractable. In March 1890 she wrote to him that she had known ever since Minneapolis that he was "deceived and deceiving others," and that he had "unsettled the minds and faith" of many in the Testimonies. Meanwhile, she publicly told the Adventist ministry not to "hang on to Brother Smith" because "he is not in the light" and hadn't been since Minneapolis. Smith especially concerned her because of his large influence in the denomination (EGW to US, Mar. 8, 1890; EGW MS 4, 1890).

For three years her efforts fell on deaf ears. Smith had dug in and would not budge. On November 25, 1890, she wrote him, "You were a man like Elder Butler—would not confess a wrong step but would make many more wrong steps to justify your first wrong step, when, if you would overcome that stubbornness that is ingrained into your life and character, the power of God would make you a man of efficiency to the very close of time." "I love you," she told him as she appealed to him to let God soften his heart and let the Spirit of Christ come in. Smith remained adamant, but he was soon to capitulate (EGW to US, Nov. 25, 1890).

In January 1891, following a Week of Prayer reading penned by Ellen White that emphasized repentance in relation to righteousness by faith, he called for a meeting with her and several leading ministers. During it he confessed many of his errors at Minneapolis. As Mrs. White put it: "He had fallen on the Rock and was broken." Taking Smith by the hand, she "told him that he had said in his confession all that he could have said." The whole experience, reported General Conference president O. A. Olsen, created "quite a sensation in Battle Creek, and the Lord is working for us in a special manner, and the way is opening up for others to clear themselves" (EGW MS 3, 1891; DTJ to RMK, Jan. 9, 1891; OAO to RAU, Jan. 16, 1891).

Smith's falling on the Rock, however, did not mean that he was altogether on the Rock. In September 1892, for example, Ellen White wrote to him: "You are not where God would have had you." He still harbored "confused ideas in regard to Christ's righteousness and justification by faith" because of the position he had taken toward Jones and Waggoner. His old theology died hard, and his Minneapolis problems fueled its continuing life. Despite his confession, he had a long way to go. Mrs. White was still asking the maturing editor to open his heart to Jesus (EGW to US, Sept. 19, 1892).

Smith not only was having difficulty surrendering his law-oriented theology, but also continued to struggle with Jones over prophetic interpretation. His inability to come to grips with the Minneapolis ideas would eventually lead to his dismissal from the editorship of the *Review* in 1897. Subsequently Jones would be editor, with Smith as his assistant.

Jones, however, did not work out as editor of the denomination's leading paper. In 1901 the church relieved him of his duties and once again appointed Smith editor in chief. Smith, as we might imagine, was overjoyed with the reversal. Surprisingly, he was not the only one delighted. *Ellen White wholeheartedly supported him despite the fact that he was still not straight on 1888-related issues.* Remarking that Smith had worked with her and her husband from the earliest days of Adventist publishing, she expressed pleasure that his name was once again at the "head of the list of editors; for thus it should be. . . . How I rejoice as I read his articles in the *Review*— so excellent, so full of spiritual truth. I thank God for them. I feel a strong sympathy for Elder Smith, and I believe that his name should always appear in the *Review* as the name of the leading editor. Thus God would have it. When, some years ago, his name was placed second [to Jones's], I felt hurt. When it was again placed first, I wept, and said, 'Thank God'" (EGW to SNH and wife, Feb. 2, 1902).

Unfortunately, Smith could not resist responding to the editorials Jones had published on the gospel in Galatians in 1900. As a result, in 1902 the "new" editor sponsored a series on Galatians that stressed the pre-1888 position on the law in Galatians with all of its theological implications. While Smith still claimed (as he did even during the 1888 period) that he believed in justification by faith, his revival of the Minneapolis controversy so upset the General Conference administration that it again removed him from the editorship. His replacement was W. W. Prescott, who had aligned himself with Jones and Waggoner in the early 1890s. The new defeat spelled the end for the aged warrior. The *Review* that announced the change also noted that he was seriously ill. Never fully recovering from the shock, he would pass to his rest in March 1903 at the age of 70.

### A. T. Jones and E. J. Waggoner

From one perspective we can view Jones and Waggoner as "victors" at Minneapolis. That is not because the conference officially accepted their views or even that many of the delegates personally adopted them. Their so-called victory was of a more modest stripe—they had been allowed to bring up the controversial topics at Minneapolis and all attempts at creedal votes had been blocked. Ellen White had supported them, and the General Conference administrations of Olsen and Irwin would back them throughout the 1890s. Of course, another perspective could see 1888 as a defeat to the reformers and their "new theology," since their teachings did not find wholehearted acceptance (see question 50 on the issue of acceptance or rejection of the 1888 message).

Immediately after the Minneapolis event Jones and Waggoner found it difficult to get a hearing. But that situation did not persist. Through the aid of O. A. Olsen, Ellen White, and others they became leading speakers in the denomination (see question 43).

We can perhaps best gauge the magnitude of the General Conference support from the central role the two men had as the featured speakers on Bible topics at the General Conference sessions in the post-Minneapolis period.

- In 1889 Jones had a series on justification by faith. The people, Ellen White noted, "are being fed with large morsels from the Lord's table" and "great interest is manifested" (EGW MS 10, 1889).

- The 1891 session (after 1889 they convened every second year) featured Waggoner and his 16 sermons uplifting Jesus Christ and the everlasting gospel in Romans.

- Jones led the Bible study sessions in 1893, with 24 sermons on the *third angel's message. Ten sermons on the promise of the Holy Spirit by W. W. Prescott—Jones's closest colleague in the United States from 1892 to the end of the century—complemented his work.*

- *The 1895 meetings again saw Jones as the leading Bible expositor, with 26 sermons on the third angel's message, besides other presentations.*

- *Waggoner's 18 studies on Hebrews were the focal point of Bible study in 1897. Jones made some 11 presentations on such topics as "The Spirit of Prophecy," "The Science of Salvation," and the call for the denomination to come out of spiritual Babylon and Egypt.*

Whatever else one might say, the General Conference leaders throughout the 1890s gave the two Minneapolis reformers front billing at the General Conference sessions.

Beyond the support of the denomination's general officers, Jones and Waggoner benefited greatly from their association with Ellen White and her generous support of their Christ-oriented approach. Repeatedly she said publicly and wrote for all to read that they were God's special messengers who had lessons on salvation that the denomination, with its law-oriented theology, desperately needed.

Jones and Waggoner, as we noted earlier, preached often with Ellen White at Adventist gatherings across the nation between 1889 and the summer of 1891. Their message was justification by faith and the righteousness of Christ. By 1892, with Mrs. White in Australia and Waggoner in Great Britain, Jones and W. W. Prescott had become the leaders of Adventism's reform element in the United States.

While Jones and Waggoner had an important message for the denomination, it is unfortunate that as the 1890s progressed they created problems by pushing certain points too far. They not only used expressions that savored of extremes, they actually took extreme positions. Mrs. White was especially concerned with the sensitive Jones, "who is so ardent in his faith, and does not manifest the caution he should in his statements by pen or voice." As a result, he often preached "to create an excitement of feeling." She cautioned him to avoid the new and startling, but that proved to be an impossible task for the creative Jones. Prescott generally followed his lead in both the extremes and the excitement (EGW to SNH, June 1, 1894; EGW to WWP and ATJ, Apr. 16, 1894). Waggoner, on the other hand, was more sedate, but he also too often followed his logic beyond the realm of balanced theology.

In spite of their individual differences, Jones, Waggoner, and Prescott tended to become involved in the same difficulties in the 1890s. Extremes in such areas as church organization, church-state relationships, faith healing, and the sponsorship of Anna Rice offer examples. But despite such problems, Ellen White stood firmly behind Jones and Waggoner and their 1888 message of righteousness by faith. Up through at least 1896 she repeatedly asserted that they were God's messengers in uplifting Christ. On the other hand, *it goes beyond the facts to infer that she approved of all their extensions of the basic message of righteousness by faith during the late 1880s and early 1890s.* In fact, as we noted earlier, she had not even agreed with all their theology or scriptural interpretations related to the issue at the 1888 meetings (see question 22).

In the early 1890s Ellen White had hinted at the possibility of Jones and Waggoner leaving the denomination. She stated: "It is quite possible that Elder Jones or Waggoner may be overthrown by the temptations of the enemy; but if they should be, this would not prove that they had had no message from God, or that the work that they had done was all a mistake" (EGW to US, Sept. 19, 1892). About that same time she cautioned Jones to "remember that there are some whose eyes are intently fixed upon you, expecting that you will over-reach the mark, and stumble and fall." She pleaded with him to keep close to Jesus in humility (EGW to ATJ, Apr. 9, 1893).

Paradoxically, it was the so-called "victors" at Minneapolis rather than the "losers" who eventually left the denomination. Waggoner's most serious problems began in England, where he began to espouse pantheistic sentiments. His pantheistic views had become quite pronounced by the time of his 1897 General Conference studies in the book of Hebrews. "God spake," he claimed, "and, lo! that Word appeared as a tree, or as grass." "Behold your God," he noted five days later. "Where?—In the things which he has made. . . . It is undeniable that there was a wonderful power manifested in that blade of grass. But what was that power?—God's own life, his own personal presence there" (1897 GCB 34, 35, 86, 87). At the 1899 session, while teaching on the topic of "The Water of Life," Waggoner claimed that "a man may get righteousness in bathing, when he knows where the water comes from" (1899 GCB 80, 53). His *Glad Tidings* (1900) had similar thoughts: "The sunlight that shines upon us, the air that we breathe, the food that we eat, and the water that we drink, are all means of conveying life to us. The life that they convey to us is none other than the life of Christ, for He is the life, and thus we have constantly before us and in us evidence of the fact that Christ can live in us" (p. 92).

Waggoner's pantheism was an extension of two principles growing out of his 1882 conversion experience (see question 3). First, he had extended his desire to find Christ everywhere in the Bible to everywhere in general—a position that found a great deal of support in the liberal element of late-nineteenth-century Protestantism with its emphasis on the immanence of God in the world. Second, and more important, he had become confused on the basic foundations of his faith. The root of his problem was his determination to "study the Bible in the light" of his subjective experience in 1882, rather than evaluating that experience by the Bible. Having lost his objective biblical base, he was open to error in every realm as he looked for Christ in all things and not just in the Bible. His pantheistic problem was further exacerbated by a theology that tended, as time went on, to put more and more emphasis on the indwelling, subjective aspects of Christ's work and progressively less on the objective aspects. Given his belief structure, Waggoner's alignment with John Harvey Kellogg against the church during the early twentieth century is not difficult to understand.

Not only did Waggoner espouse pantheism while in England,

but he began advocating the concept of "spiritual affinity"—a viewpoint that a person not rightfully a marriage partner in this life might be one in the life to come. His entanglement with Ms. Edith Adams, a British nurse, led his wife to divorce him in 1905. The next year he married Ms. Adams.

Even though Waggoner separated from denominational employment during the Kellogg schism in the early 1900s, he never became aggressive against the church or its teachings. While retaining his belief in righteousness by faith, however, he had given up many of the distinctive Adventist teachings by the time of his death in 1916.

Jones preached the funeral sermon of Waggoner, his *"blood brother* in 'the blood of the everlasting covenant'" *(Gathering Call,* November 1916). Like Waggoner, he had sided with Kellogg in the Battle Creek schism in 1903, becoming president of the doctor's new Battle Creek College.

Having been rejected in his bid for denominational leadership in the late 1890s and the early years of the twentieth century, Jones, unlike Waggoner, became the foremost public assailant of the Seventh-day Adventist denomination and Ellen White. In a series of tracts and small books he attacked church organization, the concept of a denominational president, and the person and work of Ellen White (see GRK, *From 1888 to Apostasy,* 206-256).

The church removed his ministerial credentials in 1907 and his church membership in 1909. After 1915 he edited *The American Sentinel of Religious Liberty,* a private publication that took regular public potshots at Adventists. His church affiliations were erratic during this period, his last fellowship being with a group of tongues-speaking, Sabbathkeeping Pentecostals. Unfortunately for him, they decided to organize into the abomination of abominations—a denomination—and he had to forsake them *(American Sentinel,* September, October, November 1922). Soon thereafter, his health broke down. After a lingering illness, he died in May 1923 as the last major contestant of the battles of 1888.

THEOLOGICAL
ISSUES RAISED
BY THE
MINNEAPOLIS
MEETINGS

In the past three chapters we have examined the meaning of the 1888 message and some of the repercussions of that message as the denomination moved beyond Minneapolis. In this chapter we will look at some of the most important theological issues raised by the 1888 General Conference session. (At this point we should note that while our first question in this chapter is not strictly theological, it does have theological implications that bear on some of the other topics treated.)

### 50. Was the 1888 message accepted or rejected?

That question could be answered in several ways. One is to let the proponents of the message give their own opinion. By 1893 Jones claimed that "some there accepted it; others rejected it entirely," while "others tried to stand half way between" (1893 GCB 185).

In 1899 (after a decade of preaching and writing on the topic of the 1888 message) both Jones and Waggoner were much more positive about the message's acceptance. Waggoner, for example, told the delegates to the 1899 General Conference session that the principles that he and Jones had preached at Minneapolis "have been *accepted, to a considerable extent, since that time.*" He went on to point out that the emphasis on Christ's righteousness had not destroyed, as some feared it would, the Adventist theological distinctives or the denomination's high view of the law. To the contrary, "the result is that we see more life in the law of God, and in the truth of the Sabbath, than we ever did before" (1899 GCB 94; italics supplied).

Jones reflected a similar position. Four days after Waggoner's remarks on the topic of the 1888 message having been accepted "to a considerable extent" Jones told the assembled delegates that "we used to preach the commandments of God as we thought. But we were not preaching them, indeed, as they must be. The Lord sent a message, and sent his word by that message, saying that the faith of Jesus, righteousness by faith, must be preached. He says that *he sent the message of righteousness by faith because the people had lost sight of Christ,* in the righteousness of Christ as he is. *I am afraid that there has been a tendency to go over to the other end now, and preach the faith of Jesus without the commandments.*" Jones went on to argue that Adventists needed to preach the commandments and the faith of Jesus in combination and in proper balance (RH, June 20, 1899; italics supplied).

That is truly an astounding statement. Not only did Jones agree with Waggoner that the church had largely accepted the message, but he asserted that the denomination's preachers may, in their emphasis on what was uplifted at Minneapolis, have gone too far in the direction of emphasizing the faith of Jesus, which he equated with the 1888 message of righteousness by faith.

A third witness of the theological acceptance of the 1888 message is Ellen White, Jones and Waggoner's colleague at Minneapolis and throughout the 1890s. On February 6, 1896, Mrs. White addressed a letter to "My Brethren in America," advising the discontinuance of the three- to five-month-long ministerial institutes set up in the wake of the Minneapolis crisis to educate the ministry, because they were no longer necessary. "Men," she penned, "are called from the fields, where they should have continued working in the love and fear of God, seeking to save the lost, to spend weeks in attending a ministerial institute. *There was a time when this work was made necessary, because our own people opposed the work of God by refusing the light of truth on the righteousness of Christ by faith"* (TM 401; italics supplied; cf. 6T 89).

In her statement Ellen White recognized that in the seven years since Minneapolis, the situation had changed so much that it was no longer necessary to summon ministers together for institutes to instruct them on the topic of righteousness by faith.

W. C. White highlights and reinforces that point: "Mother tells me that some of our people are making a mistake in planning institutes for the benefit of ministers and laborers. . . . *She says that after the Minneapolis conference there was much need of ministerial institutes, but now that the light has been presented and accepted, that it is the duty of those workers to gather about them younger laborers and lay helpers, and to go into the mission fields* working, and teaching as they work. We are near the end; time is short, and every effort must now be made to carry the message in the shortest time to the largest number of people" (WCW to DAR, Sept. 10, 1895; italics supplied).

*With the above statements of Waggoner, Jones, and Mrs. White in mind, it is important to note their unity of opinion on the fact that the church had accepted the 1888 message of righteousness by faith.*

Beyond those affirmations of acceptance it is important to realize that General Conference leaders made no official rejection of the message. In fact, as we have noted several times previously, the General Conference administrations of O. A. Olsen (1888-1897) and G. A. Irwin (1897-1901) did everything in their power to put Jones and Waggoner at the forefront of Adventism from 1889 up through the end of the century. Thus they were not only the featured speakers at every General Conference session during the 1890s, but they had broad access to the denomination through its publishing houses. Jones was even elevated to what was probably the most influential post in the denomination at the time—the editorship of the *Review and Herald*. It is hard to imagine more supportive administrations to the 1888 messengers. *Officials of the General Conference have given no other theologians in the history of the denomination more prominence than Jones and Waggoner.* They were anything but rejected by the post-1888 administrations.

By this time you may be wondering why with all these testimonies for acceptance some in the twentieth century have focused on the idea of rejection. The answer to that issue is varied. Part of it is that the General Conference leadership in 1888 certainly did reject the message. But then, of course, they also resigned their General Conference offices. As a result, they could no longer be counted as the official leaders of the church.

A second part of the answer is that several key leaders throughout the 1890s continued to reject the 1888 message even though the 1888 messengers and Ellen White were quite convinced that the church had largely accepted it. Many of the leaders who resisted it eventually left the church. Such was the case of Harmon Lindsay (treasurer of the General Conference who died as a Christian Scientist), Clement Eldridge (manager of the Review and Herald Publishing Association), Frank Belden, and others. Before leaving the church, these influential men (and others who remained in Adventism) represented continuing sectors of rejection. Acceptance, even at an intellectual level, has never been universal, just as rejection at the 1888 meetings had not been universal. *Ellen White's testimonies concerning those individuals who continued to resist stand behind her statements regarding continuing rejection of the message in the 1890s.* Thus she not only indicated that the denomination had generally accepted the message by 1895-1896, but she could write "in warning to those who have stood for years resisting light and cherishing the spirit of opposition." How long, she asked in 1895, would such individuals reject the 1888 message? "Many," she said in the same letter, "have listened to the truth [of the 1888 message] spoken in demonstration of the Spirit, and they have not only refused to accept the message, but they have hated the light" (TM 96, 97, 91).

A much more serious problem than blatant outward rejection of the 1888 message was the tendency on the part of some to accept the message intellectually while failing to internalize it so that it became a part of their daily life. Jones touched upon this point in 1921. In recounting his post-Minneapolis preaching tours with Ellen White and E. J. Waggoner, he pointed out that "this turned the tide with the people, and apparently with most of the leading men. But this latter was only apparent; it was never real, for all the time in the General Conference Committee and amongst others there was a secret antagonism always carried on" (ATJ to CEH, May 12, 1921). Of course, how much of that antagonism concerned righteousness by faith and how much involved other issues, such as the law in Galatians and Jones's personality, is impossible to determine. On the whole, however, it appears that his assessment of the situation is valid.

W. C. White, who certainly did not have much common ground with Jones in their later years, basically agreed with him in evaluating the post-Minneapolis experience. White wrote that "one by one, those who had been among the opposition at Minneapolis, made confession, accepted and rejoiced in the new found light, and preached it, at least theoretically." After pointing out that the message was not "generally rejected," White granted "that there was not that entering into the experience either by ministers or people, to the extent that God was calling for, and after a few years, without any open rejection or repudiation of the doctrine, a formalism and apathy prevailed" (WCW to TGB, Dec. 30, 1930).

Perhaps White's remarks hold the answer to the tension between acceptance and rejection. It is one thing to accept a doctrine theoretically and quite another to apply it to daily experience. Yet experiential application of Christ's righteousness in daily life is at the heart of the 1888 message of righteousness by faith. Jones himself may be a case in point here—at least Ellen White thought so. While she often in the early nineties commended his gospel message, later in her life she would write that he had *never yet been thoroughly converted.* You have *seen* the strait gate," she told him, "but you have *not passed through* it to the narrow way" (EGW to ATJ, Nov. 19, 1911; italics supplied). Certainly many of his character traits in the 1890s tend to validate the view that he lacked an experiential application of his own teachings.

Thus we may conclude with the various proponents of the 1888 message that by the late 1890s the church and its leaders had largely received the 1888 message. We can also conclude that many failed to transform that acceptance into practice in daily living. Of course, no amount of teaching and preaching can effect that transmission to daily practice. Putting one's Christianity into practice is the responsibility of the individual Christian as the Holy Spirit convicts him or her. Failure in that line as well as failure to accept God's message leads to the necessity for individual Christians to confess their sins and to open their hearts, minds, and lives to God's workings (for more on the acceptance or rejection of the 1888 message, see questions 44 and 49).

### 51. How many times did Ellen White call for general denominational repentance by the Seventh-day Adventist Church or its leaders in relation to the rejection of the 1888 message?

*ZERO!*

That answer is not only the shortest one in this book, but also the easiest to understand.

If Ellen White made no such call, you may be asking, then where did the idea come from? *The idea of general "denominational repentance"* (see RJW and DKS, *1888 Re-examined*, rev. ed., 19; RJW and DKS, *"An Explicit Confession . . . Due the Church"* 39-45) *for rejecting the 1888 message rests upon a human chain of logic* that takes "corporate" or denominational guilt in rejecting the 1888 message by the church as its starting point (RJW, *Corporate Repentance* 39-41). *The most serious fallacy for the theory is that there was no such thing as corporate or denominational rejection.* We noted in question 50 that not only did the post-1888 General Conference administrations support the 1888 messengers, but that Waggoner, Jones, and Ellen White agreed that by the late 1890s the church had generally accepted the 1888 message.

*A second deadly flaw to the theory of general denominational re-pentance for rejection of the 1888 message is that we have not even one quotation from Ellen White's voluminous writings on the topic of 1888 that calls for it. Such a quotation, of course, would be a gold mine for the proponents of rejection. In fact, such a quotation would end the dis-agreement on the topic;* it would prove the point. I have one book in my library totally dedicated to the topic of general denominational repentance for rejecting the message of 1888 (see RJW, *Corporate Repentance)*, but it produces no such explicit request from Ellen White. Again, one can read the four volumes of *The Ellen G. White 1888 Materials* and not find her once explicitly urging general denominational repentance for rejecting the 1888 message. Any such call must be built upon human presuppositions. That is exactly what we find in treatments on the topic. *In place of authoritative calls from Ellen White we find long strands of human reason interspersed with quotations and ideas from the Bible, Ellen White, and Adventist history—often taken out of context or built upon faulty assumptions.*

That does not mean that Ellen White never urged repentance over issues related to the rejection of the 1888 message. We find such calls for repentance, but they are aimed at those individuals who rejected the 1888 message of Christ's righteousness (see question 50). Thus she could write to F. E. Belden that "never before have I seen among our people such firm self-complacency and un-willingness to accept and acknowledge light as was manifested at Minneapolis. I have been shown that *not one* of the company who cherished the spirit manifested at that meeting would again have clear light to discern the preciousness of the truth sent them from heaven *until they humbled their pride and confessed* that they were not actuated by the Spirit of God, but that their minds and hearts were filled with prejudice. The Lord desired to come near to them, to bless them and heal them of their backslidings, but they would not hearken" (1888 Materials 1067; italics supplied).

That quotation is typical of many found urging *individuals* to repent over their rejection of the 1888 message. It goes against the historical facts and the writings of Ellen White to say that she called for general denominational repentance for corporate or denominational guilt in rejecting the 1888 message. One of the tragedies of modern Adventism is that so many have been misled on this very point. We find neither general denominational guilt nor a call for general denominational repentance in relation to Minneapolis. On the other hand, we observe much indication of individual guilt and the need for individual repentance in relation to rejecting the 1888 message. Mrs. White is clear on those points. And in that clarity she is quite in harmony with the New Testament view of salvation that Jones and Waggoner did so much to promote. Waggoner is in agreement with Ellen White on individual responsibility for rejecting the gospel message. "There can be no Christian experience," he wrote, "no faith, no justification, no righteousness, that is not an individual matter. People are saved as individuals, and not as nations" *(Gospel in Galatians* 45).

Of course, some would argue that we need general denominational repentance for having rejected the outpouring of the latter rain in 1893, which supposedly resulted in the entire church missing God's blessing. But as we saw in questions 40 and 46, Jones's impressions that God was pouring out the latter rain derived largely from his false belief in Anna Rice as a second Adventist prophet. Such a gift hardly supports his latter rain claims. Again, we should emphasize, the accusation of general denominational failure in 1893 and the need for general denominational repentance is once again a human construction. We find no condemnation from Ellen White for rejecting the latter rain in 1893. Nor do we find her calling for general denominational repentance over such a rejection. We are here again dealing with purely human interpretations built upon several false presuppositions.

## 52. What part did discussions of the human nature of Christ play at the 1888 General Conference session?

From all existing records it appears that the topic of the human nature of Christ had an extremely small role at the Minneapolis meetings. Mrs. White would later commend the 1888 message for uplifting the "divine person" of Jesus (TM 92), but we find no such commendation or mention of any discussion of Christ's human nature at Minneapolis.

That does not mean that the topic never surfaced. After all, we do have at least *one* statement on the topic. Waggoner's *Gospel in Galatians* (circulated at Minneapolis) has a paragraph that notes that "his being made in all things like unto his brethren, is the same as his being made in the likeness of sinful flesh." Waggoner went on to note that "if Christ had not been made *in all things* like unto his brethren, then his sinless life would be no encouragement to us" (p. 61).

It seems from that statement that by the time of the Minneapolis meetings Waggoner probably already held what we know was his later position on the human nature of Christ. That supposition becomes quite certain a couple of months after the 1888 session. In the *Signs of the Times* of January 21, 1889, he penned that children "are born with sinful tendencies." And, he continued, "when Christ came into the world, he came subject to all the conditions to which other children are subject."

Thus we can conclude with certainty that Waggoner believed that Christ was born with "sinful tendencies" by early 1889 and that he probably held such a view prior to the Minneapolis conference. That, of course, does not mean that at that early date the concept had a large role in his theology (we certainly have no evidence that it did) or that he was correct. In fact, his January 21, 1889, article had at least one aspect of his theology of the human nature of Christ that was definitely in error. Three times he claimed that it was impossible for Christ to commit sin, because God was in Him. Again, we should note that just because Waggoner believed something does not mean that Ellen White agreed with him. She certainly didn't on Christ's inability to sin (see question 22). We will examine what Ellen White did agree with him on regarding the human nature of Christ in question 53.

The theology set forth by Jones, Waggoner, and Prescott on the human nature of Christ evolved throughout the early 1890s. While it was not highly visible in the late 1880s and early 1890s, by 1893 and 1894 it was becoming a more important part of their theology. But it is at the 1895 General Conference session that we find Jones expressing it in its maturity. At the 1895 meetings Jones preached 26 times on the third angel's message. Those sermons contain what may be the most complete discussion by either Jones or Waggoner on the human nature of Christ in relation to righteousness by faith.

Jones laced his 1895 General Conference sermons with his view on the subject of Christ's human nature, devoting six of them to it entirely. His later writings on the topic never varied significantly from his 1895 presentations. Neither do his writings on the subject differ essentially with the ideas of Waggoner or Prescott. It therefore behooves us to spend some time examining Jones's 1895 arguments.

Without doubt, by 1895 Jones saw the total likeness of Christ's nature to that of other humans as central to his presentation of righteousness by faith. In his 1895 presentations Jones pointed out that for three or four years the denomination had been studying the meaning of Christ's emptying Himself, but that he was quite convinced that his present teachings were in advance of anything the church had previously heard on the topic (1895 GCB 330).

Jones, in his usual manner, was quite explicit as he put his beliefs before the delegates. "Christ's nature," he claimed, "is precisely our nature." "In his human nature there is not a particle of difference between him and you." Christ did not come like the first Adam, "but as the first Adam had caused his descendants to be at the time at which he came" *(ibid.* 231, 233, 436).

To get the full impact of this likeness, we need to realize that Jones had previously told the delegates that at the *"moment"* that Adam and Eve sinned they had "'total depravity.'" For Jones the Fall did not merely mar the image of God in man—it obliterated it. Adam and Eve could not tell the truth to God in Eden, because their *mind* was in bondage to Satan *(ibid.* 192, 191).

It was in this depraved human nature that Christ became like us with "not a particle of difference between him and you." There was, Jones claimed, "not a single tendency to sin in you and me that was not in Adam when he stepped out of the garden." Christ took our flesh in the Incarnation, with "just the same tendencies to sin that are in you and me. . . . All the tendencies to sin that are in human flesh were in his human flesh," yet "not one of them was ever allowed to appear; he conquered them all. And in him we all have victory over them all" *(ibid.* 233, 333, 266, 267).

Jones did not hold that Jesus was a sinner, even though at times he became careless in his language, even saying at one point that Christ "was sinful as we." His apparent carelessness in language extended beyond his 1895 General Conference sermons. In 1896, for example, he would note four times in one article that Christ had "human flesh laden with sin." Again in 1894, while preaching at the Battle Creek Tabernacle on the nature of Christ's flesh, he defined sinful flesh as being "full of sin" *(ibid.* 302; BE, Nov. 30, 1896; ATJ MS, July 14, 1894).

His use of language is often confusing. Jones's extremes in expression and thought do not help the situation. In addition to those problems, it is often impossible to tell exactly what he had in mind. For example, we can interpret many of his discussions of Christ's nature to mean that Christ took our sinful nature vicariously, just as He bore our sins on the cross vicariously when He became sin for us.

After accounting for all the careless language, exaggerations, and ambiguities in Jones's statements, however, it is still evident that he believed that Christ became incarnate in flesh just like ours, with all of its sinful tendencies. On the other hand, Jesus was without sin. He was, in fact, a demonstration to the universe that individuals can overcome sin in human flesh. Jesus is an example in this matter for every Christian. Jones stated: "In Jesus Christ as he was in sinful flesh, God has demonstrated before the universe that he can so take possession of sinful flesh as to manifest his own presence, his power, and his glory, instead of sin manifesting itself. And all that the Son asks of any man, in order to accomplish this in him, is that the man will let the Lord have him as the Lord Jesus did" (1895 GCB 303).

In other words, if persons surrender to Jesus, God will dwell in their sinful flesh today. "God will so dwell yet in sinful flesh that in spite of all the sinfulness of sinful flesh, his influence, his glory, his righteousness, his character, shall be manifested wherever that person goes." Thus Jesus "is a Saviour from sins committed, and the Conqueror of the tendencies to commit sins." Christ offers the power of his "resurrection" to every believer. In short, Jones pointed out in 1905, by overcoming sin in sinful human flesh, Jesus had opened a "consecrated way" for each of His followers to do the same. Each can have "perfection of character . . . in human flesh in this world" *(ibid.* 377, 267, 433; *Consecrated Way* 84). That, of course, he often noted, resulted not from human effort, but from the surrender of the will and from the indwelling of the Holy Spirit.

That type of living, Jones declared in 1897, would make God's people a demonstration to the universe. Their lives would proclaim: " 'Here are they that keep the commandments of God and the faith of Jesus' " (1897 GCB 279).

Not all the delegates at the 1895 General Conference session agreed with Jones's position that Christ was like fallen humanity in every way. *They challenged him with a statement from Ellen White that claims that Christ "is a brother in our infirmities, but not in possessing like passions"* (2T 202; italics supplied). Jones tried to tersely pass off the quotation, but in his next sermon he had to deal with it extensively. His way around the problem was to differentiate between Christ's flesh and His mind. "Now as to Christ not having 'like passions' with us," he claimed, "in the Scriptures all the way through he is like us, and with us according to the flesh. . . . Don't go too far. *He was made in the likeness of sinful flesh; not in the likeness of sinful mind.* Do not drag his mind into it. His flesh was our flesh; but the mind was 'the mind of Christ Jesus.' . . . If he had taken our mind, how, then, could we ever have been exhorted to 'let this mind be in you, which was also in Christ Jesus?' It would have been so already. But what kind of mind is ours? O, it is corrupted with sin" (1895 GCB 312, 327; italics supplied).

Adam and Eve, Jones explained, "forsook the mind of Jesus" and accepted that of Satan. As a result, both they *and us* were "enslaved" to that mind. Jesus came into the world with the flesh of Adam but the mind of God. He fought the battle at just the point where Adam lost—appetite. Thus He conquered Satan on his own ground, and "in Jesus Christ the mind of God is brought back once more to the sons of men; and Satan is conquered" *(ibid.* 327).

Jesus never consented to sin with His mind, Jones argued. His mind won over the flesh. Individuals can have that same mind by faith in Him through the indwelling of the Holy Spirit. They can therefore be "partakers of the divine nature." The solution is to depend upon God at all times. When individuals do this, "that mind which He gives to me will exercise in me the same faith it exercised in Him" *(ibid.* 328-331).

Jones's argument partly succeeded and partly failed in his attempt to explain how Christ's human nature did not differ "a particle" from ours, even though He did not possess our passions. A measure of success came from the fact that he managed to end his argument with Christ still possessing sinful flesh that had all the tendencies to sin experienced by every other human being. He also succeeded in that he demonstrated that the born-again Christian could have the mind of Christ through the indwelling of the Holy Spirit. The Christian, he argued, could have the same power through faith that Jesus had through faith.

*Jones's argument failed, however, in the sense that he had to admit that Jesus was not just like the non-Christian or the child who still had not accepted Christ by faith and still, therefore, possessed the fallen mind of Adam. That failure, in the last count, meant that he had denied the premise that he had started with. He had been forced to admit that Jesus had "precisely our nature" only in terms of His flesh. Our Saviour did not have our passions, because He did not have the fallen mind of Adam and Eve. Thus in the end Jones demonstrated that there really was more than "a particle of difference" between Christ and other human beings. Or, to put it bluntly, Jones proved just the opposite from what he intended.*

While he may have lost his argument, he contributed many

valuable insights, not the least of which is that a Christian can live the victorious life by being born from above by the Holy Spirit. Therein is the secret of Christian living on the order of the 1888 message. At conversion a person can have the mind of Christ, something that Christ possessed, as Jones inferred in his argument, from His birth.

### 53. How does the theology of Ellen White on the nature of Christ compare with that of Jones and his colleagues?

As we move into this topic, we should note that the issue of the human nature of Christ did not become controversial in Adventism until the mid-1950s. Up to that time the denomination's writers had fairly well agreed with Jones, Waggoner, and Prescott that Christ had come in human flesh that had, like the fallen Adam's, all of humanity's tendencies to sin.

One major stimulus for a shift in the position of several denominational thought leaders in the 1950s was the "discovery" of the "Baker letter." Coupled with that was a sensitivity to the criticism that Adventism's "sinful tendencies" Christology was less than adequate.

Ellen White penned the controversial letter to W.L.H. Baker in early February 1896. Its recipient was an ordained minister in the Central Australian Conference. Since that letter has become so important in Adventist theological discussion, we will quote it at some length. *"Be exceedingly careful,"* Ellen White wrote, *"how you dwell upon the human nature of Christ. Do not set him before the people as a man with the propensities of sin. He is the second Adam. The first Adam was created a pure, sinless being, without a taint of sin upon him; he was in the image of God. . . . Because of sin, his posterity was born with inherent propensities of disobedience. But Jesus Christ was the only begotten Son of God. He took upon himself human nature, and was tempted in all points as human nature is tempted. He could have sinned; he could have fallen, but not for one moment was there in him an evil propensity.* He was assailed with temptations in the wilderness, as Adam was assailed with temptations in Eden.

"Bro. Baker, avoid every question in relation to the humanity of Christ which is liable to be misunderstood. . . . In treating upon the humanity of Christ, you need to guard strenuously every assertion, lest your words be taken to mean more than they imply, and thus you lose or dim the clear perceptions of his humanity as combined with divinity. His birth was a miracle of God." Mrs. White then goes on to quote Luke 1:31-35, which speaks of Jesus as that "holy thing" (KJV) who had God as His Father.

"These words are not addressed to any human being, except to the Son of the Infinite God. *Never, in any way, leave the slightest impression upon human minds that a taint of, or inclination to corruption rested upon Christ,* or that he in any way yielded to corruption. He was tempted in all points like as man is tempted, yet he is called that holy thing. . . . The incarnation of Christ has ever been, and will ever remain a mystery. That which is revealed, is for us and for our children, but *let every human being be warned from the ground of making Christ altogether human, such an one as ourselves; for it cannot be. . . .*

"I perceive that there is danger in approaching subjects which dwell on the humanity of the Son of the infinite God. . . .

*"There are many questions treated upon that are not necessary for the perfection of the faith"* (EGW to Brother and Sister Baker, [Feb. 9, 1896]; italics supplied; cf. EGW MS 57, 1890, where Ellen White said that "we must not become in our ideas common and earthly, and *in our perverted ideas we must not think that the liability of Christ to yield to Satan's temptations degraded His humanity and* [that] *He possessed the same sinful, corrupt sinful propensities as man"*).

Baker replied to Mrs. White on March 6, 1896, thanking her for the letter, but without shedding any light on the exact nature of his "problem."

Since the recovery of the Baker letter a great deal of controversy has arisen over its exact meaning. Several definitions of "propensities" have been proposed. Some explanations have been ingenious, while others have been contorted. Webster's, for whatever it is worth, says that propensity is "a natural inclination or tendency;

bent." Ellen White seems, at times, to use the word in that way. In July 1889, for example, she wrote: "Satan is appealing to the lowest propensities of human nature. But these do not need cultivation. Like thistles and briars, selfishness, self-love, envying, jealousy, evil surmisings, self-esteem, will grow up luxuriantly if only left to themselves" (EGW to Elders Madison and Miller, July 23, 1889). A decade later she seemingly equated propensities with tendencies while discussing the unfallen Adam, who had "no corrupt propensities or tendencies to evil." In 1897 she made a related comment: "There should not be the faintest misgivings in regard to the perfect freedom from sinfulness in the human nature of Christ" (EGW to GAI and SNH, Nov. 1899; EGW MS 143, 1897).

We must take Ellen White's statements on Christ not having fallen humanity's propensities to sin in the context of quotations that seem to imply the opposite. For example, in December 1896 (just a few months after the Baker letter), she published in the *Review* that Christ "took upon him our sinful nature." Then again, in 1900 she wrote that "he took upon himself fallen, suffering human nature, degraded and defiled by sin." Those were not isolated statements. In both May and September 1896, for instance, she claimed that Christ took our "fallen human nature" (RH, Dec. 15, 1896; YI, Dec. 20, 1900; RH, Sept. 29, 1896; EGW to OAO, May 31, 1896).

*There is not the slightest doubt that Ellen White believed that Christ took upon Himself fallen, sinful human nature at the Incarnation. Whatever that nature consisted of, however, it is clear that it did not include any evil propensities to sin*—those "thistles and briars" of selfishness, self-love, and so on.

That position harmonizes with other statements she made over the years on the topic. Children, she pointed out, do not have an "inborn inclination" to "do service for God." To the contrary, they have "hereditary . . . tendencies to evil that must be overcome" (CT 20). Christ, by way of contrast, had a natural inclination to do right. In 1898 she wrote: *"It is not correct to say, as many writers have said, that Christ was like all children. . . . His inclination to right was a constant gratification to his parents. . . .* He was an example of what all children may strive to be. . . . *No one,* looking upon the child-like countenance, shining with animation, *could say that Christ was just like other children"* (YI, Sept. 8, 1898; italics supplied).

In *Education* she commented that humans (including children) have "a bent to evil." On the other hand, as we have already noted, Christ had a bent toward good. Human children can get their bent, or inclination, corrected only through surrendering their wills to God, being "born from above," and accepting the power of the Holy Spirit in their lives (Ed 29, 30; SC 18, 19). Then they partake of the divine nature.

Even then, however, they are still not exactly like Christ in His humanity, because they have brought into their new life their past sinful habits and their well-developed tendencies, whereas Christ never had that distorting baggage. On the other hand, after being "born from above," they have the same power that He had to eradicate those sinful habits. That is the work of sanctification or character development. All born-from-above human beings thus fight on the same ground as Christ fought. They can be thankful that "Christ did nothing that human nature may not do if it partakes of the divine nature" (ST, June 17, 1897).

Notwithstanding that encouragement, Mrs. White pointed out a paradox in 1895: (1) Despite the fact that "divine power was not given to Him in a different way to what it will be given to us," yet (2) *"we can never equal the pattern" even though "we may imitate and resemble it"* (EGW MS 21, 1895; RH, Feb. 5, 1895). That paradox may find its roots in the reality that Christ never had to be sanctified in the same way other people do, because He was unlike other children in their inborn inclination to wrong.

*In the long run Ellen White's statements, as noted above, moved in the same direction that Jones's arguments took once he had to deal with the quotation that claimed that Christ did not have our passions* (see question 52). *Each of them ended up inferring that the inclinations and/or mind of Christ in His humanity were different from those of other children.* Both Jones and Ellen White believed that Christ had "sinful nature," but Jones tried to include more in the "sinful" than she did. In that he failed in 1895, but that did not convince him to change his position. He continued to teach that Christ had sinful tendencies in His flesh, a position that Ellen White had never explicitly stated, even though people could interpret many of her statements on the subject that way if they left out or redefined other of her comments that plainly state the opposite.

Perhaps the best avenue to understanding Mrs. White's meaning of "propensities" is by seeing how one of the authors she used to prepare some of her material on the Incarnation employed the word. Henry Melvill was one of Ellen White's favorite writers. Several of her works indicate their mutual agreement on various points. The Ellen G. White Estate has her marked copy of *Sermons by Henry Melvill, B.D.* Tim Poirier, of the White Estate, has analyzed her use of him. His sermon "The Humiliation of the Man Christ Jesus," Poirier points out, is especially helpful in enabling us to understand and reconcile the apparent conflict in Ellen White's statements on the humanity of Christ. According to Melvill, the Fall had two basic consequences: (1) "innocent infirmities," and (2) "sinful propensities." "By 'innocent infirmities,'" Poirier writes, "Melvill means such things as hunger, pain, weakness, sorrow, and death. 'There are consequences [of] guilt which are perfectly guiltless. Sin introduced pain, but pain itself is not sin.' By 'sinful propensities,' . . . Melvill refers to the proneness or 'tendency' to sin. In his summary of the discussion, Melvill argues that before the Fall Adam had neither 'innocent infirmities' nor 'sinful propensities,' that we are born with both, and that Christ took the first but not the second" ("Sources Clarify Ellen White's Christology," *Ministry,* December 1989, pp. 7, 8).

In other words, Melvill held that the incarnate Christ was neither just like Adam before the Fall nor just like fallen humanity since the Fall. That appears to be the position Ellen White held. In fact, Melvill's explanation fits quite nicely her statement that Christ "is a brother in our infirmities [Melvill's 'innocent infirmities'], but not in possessing like passions [Melvill's 'sinful propensities']" (2T

202). Of course, as we noted earlier, Jones found himself forced into a similar explanation of Christ's human nature when he sought to respond to that Ellen White quotation at the 1895 General Conference session. Unfortunately, however, he later wrote as if he had never modified his position. Thus in 1905 he could still write as though Christ inherited sinful tendencies as well as innocent infirmities (see *Consecrated Way* 40, 41, 44).

Waggoner, as we noted in question 52, had taken the same position as Jones on the human nature of Christ. To Waggoner, the flesh that "He assumed had all the weaknesses and sinful tendencies to which fallen human nature is subject." According to Waggoner's explanations, human nature had inherited *"evil propensities"* that Christ must have acquired at birth if we stick to his logic. Likewise, Christ, like David, "had all the *passions* of human nature" *(Christ and His Righteousness* 26, 87, 27; italics supplied).

*In conclusion, it can be said that Ellen White and Waggoner and Jones all agreed that Jesus was born with a sinful nature, but the two men both included inherited sinful passions and propensities in that inheritance while Ellen White excluded them.* Beyond that, she explicitly stated that it was "not correct to say, as many writers have said [including Jones and Waggoner], that Christ was like all children" (YI, Sept. 8, 1898). *Thus by the mid-1890s Jones and Waggoner had developed a theology built on a concept that directly contradicted Ellen White.*

Before we move away from the topic of Christ's human nature, it is important to note (as Woodrow Whidden's *Ellen White on the Humanity of Christ* has demonstrated) that in spite of those individuals who have tried to convince us that Christ's humanity was one of the central issues in Ellen White's great emphasis on salvation flowing out of the 1888 General Conference session, anyone who reads the four-volume *Ellen G. White 1888 Materials* will discover that *she has relatively little to say on the topic in all her discussion on Minneapolis and its aftermath* (see Whidden, p. 40).

Likewise, while she briefly comments on His human nature, one looks in vain for entire chapters on the topic of Christ's post-Fall human nature in the great books on Christ and salvation that she published in the 17 years after Minneapolis. Where, we might ask, is the chapter in *The Desire of Ages* on the human nature of Christ? Or where is the chapter in *Steps to Christ* that tells us how the topic fits into the plan of salvation? *To put it mildly, the subject of the post-Fall human nature of Christ wasn't a major agenda item in Ellen White's understanding of either how people are saved or last-day events.*

### 54. Is there in Ellen White's writings, as there is in the publications of some Adventists, a strong connection between righteousness by faith and final events?

No! In fact, the loud cry statement of 1892 (see question 39) is apparently the only place she explicitly ties the teaching of righteousness by faith to end-time events.

Whereas some authors have written multiplied books on the topic, according to the extensive doctoral research of Ralph Neall *the 1892 loud cry statement is the only time in her post-1888 writings in which "she referred to righteousness by faith . . . in connection with the final events."* Beyond that, Neall points out, *none of her comments on the delay of Christ's coming being conditional upon the church's response even mentions righteousness by faith.* Neall found that from Mrs. White's viewpoint "the Sunday law problem in 1888 pointed to Christ's coming much more than did the emphasis on righteousness by faith" *(How Long, O Lord?* 101, 102; italics supplied).

Once again we find a case in which some of Ellen White's interpreters with an interest in the 1888 message, influenced by the presentations of the misled Jones and Prescott at the 1893 General Conference session (see questions 40, 46 and 47), have developed emphases not present in her writings but quite in harmony with their own agenda based on faulty concepts of corporate guilt and denominational repentance (see questions 50 and 51).

Another point that we should note before moving away from this topic is that *those things that Ellen White repeatedly praised in the "most precious message" of Jones and Waggoner had to do with their soteriology (that is, how people are saved from sin and its penalty) rather than their eschatology (that is, their ideas of final events).* It is important to emphasize what she commended in their message (see TM 91-93 and questions 1 and 17). *Unfortunately, many feel a burden to import their own theological concerns into what she endorsed in the 1888 message.*

## 55. Is the 1888 message the message of 1888, or the message of 1893, 1895, or some other date?

This is a crucial question, because Jones and Waggoner's theology changed and developed markedly over time. That is, they included more things in their message as time went on—ideas that they did not emphasize or even preach in 1888.

*It is of the utmost importance to realize that we find Ellen White repeatedly emphasizing the necessity of restoring Christ and salvation by faith in His merits to the Adventist message, while never once explicitly endorsing such teachings as that by Jones on the beginning of the latter rain in 1893 or the teachings of Jones and Waggoner on the human nature of Christ that they had fully developed by 1895.* In fact, we saw in questions 40, 46, 52, and 53 that their teachings in these areas did not harmonize with her own ideas.

The truth is that *for Ellen White the 1888 message is the message of 1888 rather than the message of 1893 or 1895.*

At this point someone may be asking, If the above conclusion is correct, why did Ellen White continue to commend Jones and Waggoner's teachings up through 1896? The answer to that question is not difficult to come by. *Read her statements.* Adventists through those years (and on into our day) still needed to place Jesus and faith in His saving sacrifice at the center of their message as they presented a package that unified both law and gospel. What she approved of in their message in 1896 had essentially the same emphasis as in 1888. Her commendation did not reflect Jones and Waggoner's additions to their message that had developed in the 1890s.

*It is being unfaithful to her emphases to conclude that just because she still supported Jones and Waggoner in the mid-1890s, she agreed with all their teachings, unless she explicitly broadens her commendations to the new points the men had begun stressing.* We need to remember that Ellen White didn't even accept all they were teaching at Minneapolis. From what we have seen in the past few chapters, she had even more areas of disagreement with them by the mid-1890s, when both men had begun to develop ideas that would eventually lead them to sever their connections with Adventism (see question 22). *Let Ellen White speak for herself. We have too many people with an interest in the 1888 message putting ideas into her head through the avenue of their own logic and agenda.*

## 56. What is the most important lesson for "doing theology" that can be learned from the 1888 experience?

That vital lesson is the same one that Jones, Waggoner, and Ellen White tried to teach at Minneapolis regarding the all-important place of the Bible in our study. Waggoner put it succinctly when he wrote that "I do not consider the statement of any man on earth as of sufficient weight to help establish any point of doctrine. The word of God alone can decide what is right; it alone can establish a point of doctrine; and when it has spoken, nothing that any man can say can make the case any stronger. And when a thing cannot be proved by the Bible, it cannot be proved by what any man says, no matter how good he is" *(Gospel in Galatians* 66).

As noted in question 14, Ellen White was of the same mind. She constantly pounded home the role of the Bible in doctrinal formation.

There was much plain talk on religious authority at Minneapolis. Yet it is at that very point that many with an interest in the 1888 message make a serious mistake (for more on this topic, see question 26). In one of the great paradoxes of Adventist history, Jones and Waggoner, who did so much to displace the human theological authority of Smith and Butler at Minneapolis, soon found themselves being placed in the same role as their antagonists. Thus Ellen White could lament the fact that men who had "been chosen of God to do a special work have been imperiled because the people have looked to the men in the place of looking to God" (EGW to SNH, June 1, 1894). To the Battle Creek church she wrote: "The Lord has given Brother Jones a message to prepare a people to stand in the day of God; but when the people shall look to Elder Jones instead of to God, they will become weak instead of strong" (EGW to Brethren and Sisters, Mar. 16, 1894).

That truth holds true for today. *The common denominator of every theological misunderstanding related to Minneapolis discussed in this chapter is the methodology that does theology through the eyes of Jones and Waggoner. As recently as 1987 an influential book linked Jones and Waggoner together with Ellen White as "the inspired trio" (1888 Re-examined, rev. ed., 75). Such an identification tends to confound the men with their gospel message.* Beyond that, and more important, it perpetuates one of the foundational problems of Minneapolis—the need for Adventists to get back to the Bible as the only standard of doctrine and practice. Mrs. White stood firmly behind Jones and Waggoner because of their plea for openness in Bible study and their Bible-based emphasis on Christ's righteousness. She summoned Adventists to become involved in dedicated Bible study in the same way that the young reformers of 1888 were. To fixate on their words and to read the Bible through their eyes is merely to repeat the mistake of the post-Reformation era as the second and third generations approached their Bibles in the light of the sixteenth-century Reformers. The great call of 1888 was for Adventists to move away from such false paths and to become active in intense, Spirit-guided study of the Scriptures. *The challenge is to expand and enrich the theological beachhead of Jones and Waggoner, not to canonize it.*

# CHAPTER 9

# THE MEANING OF THE 1888 MESSAGE FOR TODAY

The church needs today, more than ever, the "most precious message" uplifted at Minneapolis more than a century ago. This closing chapter will highlight its contemporary importance for both the church and our individual lives. Unlike previous chapters, organized in the form of questions and answers, this chapter sets forth its ideas in the form of propositions.

**Proposition 1: Adventism needs to make Jesus and His saving righteousness central.**

The core of the 1888 message as Ellen White saw it was to uplift Jesus and full salvation in Him. Her writing ministry literally transformed as she more fully comprehended the great need for both individuals and the church to put Jesus and His saving righteousness at the center of their beliefs and lives. It resulted in such books as *The Desire of Ages* and *Steps to Christ*.

"The great Center of attraction, Jesus Christ," she penned in 1894, "must not be left out of the third angel's message. By many who have been engaged in the work for this time, Christ has been made secondary, and theories and arguments have had the first place" (RH, Mar. 20, 1894). On another occasion she wrote that "our churches are dying for the want of teaching on the subject of righteousness by faith in Christ, and on kindred truths" (GW 301).

Doctrines may be good and true, but they are meaningless outside of a saving relationship with Jesus. The church and its members must constantly keep at the forefront the fact that doctrinal truth—truth with a small "t"—is Christian truth only when it is placed in the framework of Jesus and His sacrifice and ministry. He is "the way, and the truth, and the life." No one "comes to the Father" except through Him (John 14:6, RSV). He is the *Truth* with a capital "T." All other truths are true only as they relate to Him.

Jesus is the great need of the church today, just as He was in 1888. As Ellen White so nicely put it, "Christ crucified" must be the center of our message. "Talk it, pray it, sing it, and it will break and win hearts. Set, formal phrases, the presentation of merely argumentative subjects, is productive of little good. The melting love of God in the hearts of the workers will be recognized by those for whom they labor. Souls are thirsting for the water of life. Do not allow them to go from you empty. Reveal the love of Christ to them. Lead them to Jesus, and he will give them the bread of life and the water of salvation" (RH, June 2, 1903).

## Proposition 2: Adventists need to recognize that the good news is better than most people think.

Central to the 1888 message is the fact that the gospel is truly "good news." It is not only good news, but better news than many can even imagine.

Elements of the better-than-imagined news are (1) that Jesus died for every person, even the worst possible sinner (Heb. 9:12; 10:10); (2) that He offers every individual salvation as a free gift (Eph. 2:8-10); (3) that God doesn't passively wait for sinners to desire the gift of salvation, but actively seeks them out before they sense any need (Luke 19:10; 15:4, 8, 20); (4) that He justifies or counts as righteous those who respond to His grace in faith (Rom. 3:24-26); (5) that He not only justifies such individuals, but simultaneously transforms their hearts and minds in the new birth experience and writes His law in their hearts, so that living according to His principles will be a part of their new covenant experience (John 3:3, 6; 2 Cor. 5:17; Heb. 8:8-12); (6) that He adopts as many as accept His gift of grace into His family (John 1:12); (7) that He provides His children with the empowering presence of the Holy Spirit so that they need not fall short in living the Christlike life; and (8) that He even provides the gift of faith in order that individuals may grasp His own gracious gifts made possible through the cross of Christ. (For more on the gospel themes of 1888 in the words of Waggoner and Ellen White, review questions 30 through 33.)

These great gospel themes of the 1888 message must infiltrate the preaching of Adventism. They need to form the context for the preaching of every doctrine and every ethical injunction. We need to shout the fact that the gospel is truly good news from Adventist housetops.

## Proposition 3: Adventist Christianity must move beyond the intellectual level to the experiential.

"Christianity" that is merely head knowledge is not genuine Christianity at all. It is all too easy for us, as a church and as individuals, to think that just because we have responded to the Holy Spirit and put Christ rather than mere doctrines at the center of our belief system, we have somehow arrived at the real thing. What has really happened is that we have taken only the first step in the right direction. It is one thing to put Christ at the center of our belief system and verbally accept justification by faith and the transforming, sanctifying concept of the Holy Spirit, but it is quite another actually to live the Christlike life. Every Christian is to become a conduit for God's grace and love (see, e.g., Matt. 5:7-9; 6:14, 15; 18:21-35; 25:31-46).

"A revival of true godliness among us," Ellen White penned in 1887, "is the greatest and most urgent of all our needs. To seek this should be our first work" (RH, Mar. 22, 1887). It is still our greatest need. There is no such thing as the merely justified Christian. At the very point of time in which God justifies a person, He also transforms him or her through new birth and sets the individual apart for holy use (that is, He sanctifies them). Thenceforth God's new child is to live the life of God's love as illustrated in the life and teachings of Jesus.

In *The Desire of Ages* we read that "the greatest deception of the human mind in Christ's day was that a mere assent to the truth constitutes righteousness. In all human experience a theoretical knowledge of the truth has been proved to be insufficient for the saving of the soul. It does not bring forth the fruits of righteousness. . . . The darkest chapters of history are burdened with the record of crimes committed by bigoted religionists. . . .

"The same danger still exists. Many take it for granted that they are Christians, simply because they subscribe to certain theological tenets. But they have not brought the truth into practical life. . . . They have not received the power and grace that come through sanctification of the truth. Men may profess faith in the truth; but if it does not make them sincere, kind, patient, forbearing, heavenly-minded, it is a curse to its possessors, and through their influence it is a curse to the world" (pp. 309, 310).

If our daily lives don't express our version of the "truth" in terms of loving, Christlike concern for those around us, it is because we have not yet found the *Truth* as it is in Jesus (John 13:35); it is because we still haven't discovered the Jesus of Minneapolis that Ellen White so desperately sought to present to the assembled delegates. Her burden was not merely to uplift the cross of Christ and justification through His merits, but also to help her hearers put away the spirit of the Pharisees and to let God's love flavor all they did. Christianity is not genuine unless it shapes all the affairs of daily life. "A revival of true godliness" is still the church's greatest need.

**Proposition 4: Adventists need to understand the true nature of character perfection both intellectually and experientially.**

For various reasons, some better than others, many students of the 1888 message have tied it to character perfection. Thus we need to spend some time with that concept. Beyond that, the topic has a direct relationship to the flow of material in this chapter.

For too long have Adventists thought of character perfection in terms of a list of do's and don'ts (especially don'ts). Thus they tie character perfection to such issues as healthful living, the way one observes the Sabbath, or how one dresses. Some even think they can develop a perfect character by avoiding all evil and sin. But that is not the biblical idea of character perfection. In the Bible and the writings of Ellen White, character perfection is not a negative but a positive (see, e.g., Matt. 12:43-45). It is not some evil that we avoid, but a quality of life expressed in daily living.

Perhaps the Sermon on the Mount, in which Jesus tells us that we "must be perfect" even as our "heavenly Father is perfect" (Matt. 5:48, RSV), best expresses this idea. Jesus had been building toward that conclusion ever since Matthew 5:21 in His six illustrations that move sin beyond outward actions (such as murder or adultery) to spiritual attitudes and motives. In doing this, Jesus deepened and broadened the meaning of the law beyond the mere obedient action level in an attempt to help us glimpse its inner core of love to God and other people (see Matt. 22:36-40; Rom. 13:8-10; Gal. 5:14).

The climax of His deepening and broadening of our understanding of the law comes in Matthew 5:43-48. There He tells us that we even need to love our enemies and those who persecute us (verse 44) *"so that" we may be children of our heavenly Father* (verse 45). Our Father "makes his sun rise on the evil and on the good, and sends rain on the just and the unjust" (verse 46, RSV). That is, God expresses His love to both those who respect Him and those who hate Him. Can we do the same? Can we be like our Father? It is not enough to want the best for only those with whom we are on good terms. Even the tax collectors and other "evil" people do that (verses 46, 47). Christ commands us to be perfect in love to all people, just as our Father is perfect in love (verse 48).

Now, that is pretty perfect. In my life I have gotten the victory over stopping a lot of destructive things, such as eating between meals and wasting away my day in front of the television. That I can do by sheer willpower (works), but it takes God's grace for me to love all my enemies all the time in both thought and action. I am having a hard enough time loving those I have to live and work with, let alone my enemies. In my failures I am redirected to Jesus again and again for both His forgiving and empowering grace (1 John 1:9). Oh, how we need the Jesus of Minneapolis not only to justify us but to cleanse our hearts and minds so that we might be more like the God who "so loved the world that he gave his only Son" to die in our place that we might have eternal life (John 3:16, RSV). Paul tells us that "Christ died for the ungodly" (Rom. 5:6, RSV). He died for His enemies (verses 9, 10). Could I do that?

The Bible plainly teaches that character perfection is not what we stop doing. Rather, it is becoming like the Father in outgoing, sacrificial love. It is becoming like God in character. Such things as better health are instrumental to developing a Christian character, a truth illustrated by the fact that most of us are not the best lovers when we have a sour stomach. Lifestyle attributes are not at the center of character or character perfection. They are means to an end, not the end itself. The end is being like God in mature love. Luke makes that clear in his version of the Sermon on the Mount when he parallels Jesus' command to be merciful with Matthew's being perfect. Luke 6:36 (at the end of Luke's presentation of loving one's enemies [verse 27ff.]) makes that point explicit when Jesus tells us to "be merciful, even as your Father is merciful" (RSV). Thus the Gospels equate being merciful with being perfect. Jesus knew what character was all about.

Ellen White was of the same mind. For too long have people ripped her quotations on the topic of character perfection out of their literary contexts and then attached a list of do's and don'ts in their attempt to supply an answer as to what God expects. It is much better to let Ellen White speak for herself, just as we must let Jesus speak for Himself in the Sermon on the Mount.

Take, for example, her statement about character perfection in *Christ's Object Lessons:* "Christ is waiting with longing desire for the manifestation of Himself in His church. When the character of Christ shall be perfectly reproduced in His people, then He will come to claim them as His own" (p. 69).

Too many people have read that statement without carefully examining its context. As a result, they have imputed meanings to it that one does not find in the passage itself. The two previous pages make her intent clear. She plainly states that Christ is seeking to reproduce Himself in the hearts of others, and that those who have accepted Him will have put away the self-centered living of Satan's kingdom. Instead, they will be serving others, telling others of God's goodness, and doing good. They are becoming more like Christ because they have received "the Spirit of Christ—the Spirit of unselfish love and labor for others." As a result, she says to her readers, *"your love [will] be made perfect. More and more you will reflect the likeness of Christ in all that is pure, noble, and lovely"* (pp. 67, 68). *Thus to reproduce the character of Christ perfectly is to let Him live out His love in our daily lives.*

Another of Ellen White's major statements on character perfection makes it equally clear that she is in harmony with the biblical concept of perfection. "Love," she penned, "is the basis of godliness. Whatever the profession, no man has pure love to God unless he has unselfish love for his brother. But we can never come into possession of this spirit by *trying* to love others. What is needed is the love of Christ in the heart. When self is merged in Christ, love springs forth spontaneously. The completeness of Christian character is attained when the impulse to help and bless others springs constantly from within—when the sunshine of heaven fills the heart and is revealed in the countenance.

"It is not possible for the heart in which Christ abides to be destitute of love. If we love God because He first loved us, we shall love all for whom Christ died" (COL 384).

That is the kind of experience that those who have met the Jesus of Minneapolis may have. They not only respond in grateful love to His forgiveness of their sins, they also choose to let Him live out His life of love in them through the power of the Holy Spirit. More and more they seek that maturity in Christian love which lies at the heart of biblical character development. Such men and women will find the practical godliness that Mrs. White felt so strongly about Adventists needing in the 1880s.

And in this concept we discover the answer to those who are questioning what kind of characters God's end-time people must have as they pass though the great conflict set forth in Revelation 12:17-14:16. "The last message of mercy to be given to the world," we read in *Christ's Object Lessons,* "is a revelation of His character of love. The children of God are to manifest His glory. In their own life and character they are to reveal what the grace of God has done for them" (pp. 415, 416).

Praise God for the Jesus of Minneapolis. He not only died for us and forgives us, but allows us to become channels of His mercy. He wants to live out His law in all its aspects in us.

What a tragedy that so many of the delegates at the 1888 General Conference session did not open themselves to the message of God's love and grace. In their resistance to the Holy Spirit and in their bickering over doctrine they not only acted in the mean-spiritedness of the Pharisees, but they missed out on God's blessing. That tragedy is still a potential one for us more than 100 years later. Thus we need to be open to the Spirit's leading, to what God wants to accomplish for us and in us. The secret of latter rain power lies in our willingness to surrender our hearts and lives to the infilling of God's unifying love.

## Proposition 5: Adventists need to move beyond the spirit of Minneapolis and learn to work together.

It was a lack of practical godliness that spelled disaster for Adventism at the Minneapolis meetings. Adventists knew how to contend with one another (and others) over doctrinal and personality issues, but they didn't know how to learn humbly from one another or how to work together in Christian respect and love with those who differed from them.

Ellen White in the years after Minneapolis had a never-ending burden for the need of love, forbearance, and unity among the leaders and members of the Adventist Church. Satan, she claimed, "has a hellish jubilee" "when he can divide brethren" (EGW MS 24, 1892). That, she pointed out in late 1888, had been his tactic at the recent General Conference session. She had counseled Butler at that time that he must learn to accept some variation in belief and methods of work, that he must learn to appreciate those who differed from him on what he might imagine to be the central pillars of the faith (EGW to GIB, Oct. 14, 15, 1888). One of the fruits of the spirit of Minneapolis was that the factions at the 1888 meetings found it next to impossible to cooperate during the 1890s.

Mrs. White had raised that issue at Minneapolis on October 21. The older leaders and ministers, she indicated, should humble themselves and listen to those whom God had appointed to rescue basic Christian truth from its companionship with error. They could use the fresh spiritual insight of the younger men. Also, they must learn to back off and share some of their responsibilities with the upcoming generation. Meanwhile, the younger ministers and leaders must treat "the aged workers with tenderness, as fathers," and look up to them "as counselors and guides. Young workers should respect the age and experience of their older brethren." Thus one of the great lessons of Minneapolis was that the two sides needed each other. Working together, they could have had both the fresh insight of youth and the wise counsel of age, along with the depth of understanding that comes when a variety of perspectives go into formulating denominational positions. That possibility, of course, had been fractured by the spirit of Minneapolis (EGW MS 8a, 1888).

Those who do not learn the lessons of history are bound to repeat them. Problems caused by the two factions not cooperating together were evident on several occasions during the early 1890s. One of the most serious was when A. T. Jones and W. W. Prescott set forth Anna Rice as a second Adventist prophet in 1893 and 1894 (see question 46). Stephen N. Haskell pointed out that the two younger men had not been through the early development of Adventism, and had not experienced the fanaticism related to spiritual gifts. "Had they consulted with Uriah Smith and some of those who have been in the background, and are looked upon as being 'out of date,' it would have saved them from the mistake" (SNH to EGW, Apr. 20, 1894).

Ellen White shared much the same opinion as Haskell regarding the need for the various Adventist leadership cliques that had existed since Minneapolis to cooperate, but she placed the primary blame on Smith and the old guard. They, she declared, were to a large degree responsible for the crisis, because they had held back from uniting in labor with the younger leaders. The older men had blocked the wheels of "the chariot of truth" when they should have been helping to push it. "The Lord's work needed every jot and tittle of experience that he had given Eld. Butler and Eld. Smith." God in His providence, she claimed, had allowed the situation to show the older leaders their error in not uniting with the dynamic Jones and Prescott. "Truth is always aggressive" (EGW to SNH, June 1, 1894).

Not only did the conservative older men need the enthusiastic younger leaders, but the opposite was also true. Ellen White wrote to Jones that he should not depreciate any of God's workers. Rather, he should respect "the old disciples who are the warriors of the faith" and who had experienced the difficulties in establishing the denomination in the early days. He lacked their insight and experience (EGW to ATJ, June 7, 1894).

*One of the important lessons of Minneapolis for our day is that the church is healthiest and most secure when its differing groups learn to cooperate and listen to one another.* No faction has all the truth, and no one segment is totally in error. We are strongest when we learn to work with one another in maximizing the insights and strengths of each perspective. Such a state of affairs, of course, can take place only when we assimilate the lessons of Minneapolis. Two of those central lessons are to treat one another in the spirit of Christian love and to put Christ and His Word at the center of our dialogue and endeavor.

**Proposition 6: Adventism needs to put the Bible at the very center of its theological methodology.**

This proposition should seem self-evident, since it is the one that our pioneers started out with in the 1840s. But, as we discovered in question 14, after only 40 years of history the denominational leaders were already leaning on authorities other than the Bible to settle their theological differences. Those alternate authorities included denominational tradition, creedal legislation, expert opinion, and authoritative position. We also saw in question 14 that Ellen White sought to direct the denomination's leaders away from the practice of using her own writings to solve their biblical difficulties. "The Bible is the only rule of faith and doctrine," she penned in July 1888 (RH, July 17, 1888). Five months later she wrote to Butler that "the Bible, the Bible alone, laid up in the heart and blessed by the Spirit of God, can make man right and keep him right" (EGW to GIB and wife, Dec. 11, 1888). The need for Adventists to uplift Christ and the Bible was vital in 1888, and it is vital today.

Adventism will be strong only as it focuses on God's Word in Scripture. The church needs to read the Bible through the eyes of Moses, John, Paul, and the other Bible writers rather than through the eyes of any other source, including its theologians and leaders. Yet a serious problem, as we noted in questions 26 and 56, is that some today would have us read the Bible through the eyes of Jones and Waggoner. Such a practice may be the most perilous mistake of some with an interest in the 1888 message. Ellen White upheld both men because they were leading Adventism back to Christ and the Bible, not because they had the final word on theology or even had a theology with which she fully agreed (see question 22). As we have seen repeatedly in this study, Ellen White not only supported their pointing men and women to Jesus and His righteousness, but also did not hesitate to say that the church would become weak when it looked to Jones rather than to God (EGW to Brethren and Sisters, Mar. 16, 1894). In a similar vein, she wrote to Jones and Prescott in the wake of the Anna Rice crisis that "Satan would like nothing better than to call minds away from the word" (EGW to WWP and ATJ, Apr. 16, 1894).

The advice of Jones, Waggoner, and Ellen White in 1888 is still of utmost importance today. We must put Jesus and His Word at the very center of our faith and experience.

## Proposition 7: In studying the 1888 message, Adventists need to focus on those aspects of the theology of Jones and Waggoner that Ellen White explicitly commended.

Closely related to proposition 6 with its emphasis on biblical authority is the fact demonstrated repeatedly throughout this study that Jones and Waggoner's "most precious message" finds significance in Adventism today because of Ellen White's enthusiastic and repeated endorsement (see question 17).

That support was not a blank theological check, however. Rather it was an endorsement of the fact that they were uplifting Jesus Christ and His saving grace within the context of the third angel's message. Jones and Waggoner, as repeatedly demonstrated in this volume, developed many ideas that Ellen White not only failed to approve explicitly, but that actually contradicted her positions (see questions 50, 51, 53, 54, 55, 56, 18, 22, 23, 25, 26, 28, 33, 40, and 46). *Thus it is important to concentrate on those aspects of their theology that Ellen White explicitly commended rather than on those points that have come to the forefront because of special interest groups with their own agendas in the twentieth century.*

## Proposition 8: Adventism needs to recapture the centrality of the third angel's message to its identity and forcefully preach a balanced message of law and gospel in their end-time context.

The understanding that has driven Seventh-day Adventist missionaries to the far corners of the earth is that Adventism is a special, called-out, end-time people with the divinely assigned task of preaching the message of the three angels of Revelation 14:6-12 "to every nation and tribe and tongue and people" (verse 6, RSV; cf. Rev. 10:11).

Especially crucial in that understanding has been Revelation 14:12. From its very beginning the denomination has taught that God's last-day people needed to await the arrival of their Lord from heaven patiently in spite of their disappointments in the 1840s and their frustrated hopes in the decades since that time. In addition, from its inception Seventh-day Adventism has preached that God's last-day people would keep *all* of God's commandments (including the Sabbath command) while they patiently waited for the Lord of the harvest. The earliest Adventists understood those parts of the third angel's message.

What was not so well understood in Adventism's preaching of Revelation 14:12 was the "faith of Jesus." That part of the text became the focal point of the Minneapolis General Conference meetings in 1888 as Ellen White, A. T. Jones, and E. J. Waggoner stressed an understanding of faith in the great sacrifice of Jesus on Calvary as the sin-pardoning Saviour as the missing link in Seventh-day Adventism's final message to the world (see questions 30, 31, 37, and 39). That insight, as Mrs. White and Waggoner repeatedly asserted, was not some new truth about salvation or justification by faith that the 1888 messengers discovered, but the same salvation message preached by Jesus, Paul, and the great Reformers (see question 28).

The 1888 messengers linked the preaching of law and gospel within the framework of the end-time context of Revelation 14. Or, as Ellen White put it, Jones and Waggoner had rediscovered the old truth of the gospel and had placed it in its proper framework in the third angel's message (EGW MS 8a, 1888).

*The function of Adventism hasn't changed since 1888. It is still a called-out people to preach the loud cry message that uplifts law and gospel in their proper relationship as the world moves ever more swiftly toward its final harvest.* But Adventism faces the temptation to forget that commission. It faces the temptation of settling down and becoming just another denomination among many. If and when it does so, it will have stepped off the platform that provides its identity and its reason for existing as a separate religious body. Thus a major implication of the 1888 message is a call for Adventism to remain faithful to its original goals as it preaches God's full-orbed message of the commandments of God and the faith of Jesus to the ends of the earth.

## Proposition 9: Adventists need to quit bickering with each other over the 1888 message and focus their energies on preaching the messages of the three angels to all the earth.

The amount of energy and money that Adventists spend in trying to convince each other of their various interpretations of the 1888 message must amaze the angels. But if I were the devil, that is the way I would engineer things. After all, if I could get Adventists to expend a large share of their energy and "ammunition" on each other, I would have less to worry about.

We as Adventists ought to take Ellen White more seriously. In the mid-1890s she urged an end to the annual ministerial institutes that the church had created to enlighten the Adventist ministry on the issues raised at Minneapolis. "There was a time," she penned, when these institutes were "necessary, because our own people opposed the work of God by refusing the light on the righteousness of Christ by faith" (6T 89; cf. TM 401). By the late 1890s, however, she, her son, and Jones and Waggoner all agreed that the church had largely accepted the message on at least the intellectual level (see question 50).

Ellen White's burden was clear in the mid-nineties. Adventists had spent enough time presenting the Minneapolis issues to each other. It is true that not everyone had accepted the message, but from her perspective further preaching on the topic by Adventists to each other would bring diminishing results. As W. C. White put it: "Mother tells me that some of our people are making a mistake in planning institutes for the benefit of ministers and laborers. . . . She says that after the Minneapolis conference there was much need of ministerial institutes, but now that the light has been *presented* and *accepted,* that it is the duty of those workers to gather about them younger laborers and lay helpers, and *to go into the mis-*

*sion fields* working, and teaching as they work. We are near the end; time is short, and every effort must now be made to carry the message in the shortest time to the largest number of people" (WCW to DAR, Sept. 10, 1895; italics supplied). While not all had greeted the 1888 message with open arms, enough had accepted it sufficiently for the denomination to move forward in its primary mission of preaching the distinctive messages of the three angels to all the world. If that was good counsel in the late 1890s, it seems to be even more appropriate a century later. *Perhaps it is time to put our less-than-inspired agendas to one side and to take Ellen White's counsel on the topic more seriously.*